GROWTH SEMINAR

There's Always More: Expecting New Fire

SR. NANCY KELLAR, S.C.

Surrender Prayer

Come to Me, My friend.
I call you to a deeper surrender of yourself.
I call you to come to Me.
I call you to come to My freedom.
Unloose your heart,
Surrender again to Me today.
Come to Me, My friend.
I will give you all you need.
Believe and trust in Me.
I know you will not understand.
Only know My way is the perfect way,
My plan is a perfect plan for your life.
Turn yourself to Me again today.
I wish to deepen My life in you.
I wish to give you My love.
My friend, I want to transform you
   to make you a new creation,
     ever new, ever changing.
I want to bring you into a
   deeper truth, a deeper freedom.
I want you to believe in My power
   to transform you, to heal you.
Do not limit what I can do—
   There is still so much MORE
I want to do with you and through you.
I call you to a deeper faith
  that I may be still
  more powerful in you.

          —Father Jim Ferry
            1931–1989

Growth Seminar—
There's Always More: Expecting New Fire

Fan into flame the gift of God…. God did not give us a spirit of timidity, but the Spirit of power and love and self-control. (2 Tim 1:6-7)

With gratitude to Fr. Jim Ferry who led me to expect "more" of the Holy Spirit, to Sr. Marjorie Walsh, S.C. who took the first steps into that "more" of the Spirit with me, and to the Sisters of Charity in my Charismatic House of Prayer in Scarsdale, New York, who continue to walk in the Spirit with me.

National Service Committee
Chariscenter USA
P.O. Box 628
Locust Grove, VA 22508-0628

Nihil Obstat: Msgr. William B. Smith, STD
Censor Librorum
Imprimatur: ✠ Most Reverend Robert A. Brucato
Vicar General, Archdiocese of New York

The *Nihil Obstat* and the *Imprimatur* are official declarations that a book or pamphlet is free of doctrinal or moral error. No implication is contained therein that those who have granted the *Nihil Obstat* or *Imprimatur* agree with the contents, opinions or statements expressed.

Except where noted, Scripture from *The New Jerusalem Bible* © 1985 by Doubleday, a division of Random House, Inc. and Darton, Longman & Todd, LTD.

Where noted, Scripture texts in this work are taken from the *New American Bible* © 1970 Confraternity of Christian Doctrine, Washington, DC and are used by permission of the copyright owner. All Rights Reserved. No part of the *New American Bible* may be reproduced in any form without permission in writing from the copyright owner.

Excerpts from the English translation of the *Catechism of the Catholic Church* for use in the United States of America Copyright 1994, United States Catholic Conference, Inc. – Libreria Editrice Vaticana. Used with permission.

Copyright 2002 by Sr. Nancy Kellar, S.C.
Fifth Printing
ISBN 0-9677377-1-0

Growth Seminar—
There's Always More: Expecting New Fire

Foreword 7
Preparaton for Teachers 8

I. More Love

1. Expecting More of the Fire of the Holy Spirit 19
    A. **Desire**: More of the promises for personal renewal 19
    B. **Detachment**: Be emptied of the obstacles to growth 20
    C. **Dependence**: Surrender anew to the release of the Spirit 21

2. More Love Through Prayer 23
    A. Be **Available** to the Father's recreating love 23
    B. Be **Vulnerable** to Jesus' healing love 25
    C. Be **Expectant** of the Spirit's sanctifying love 27

3. More Love Through Purification 29
    A. The **Truth**: Recognize and overcome misconceptions 29
    B. The **Way**: Acknowledge and accept that purification leads to maturity 31
    C. The **Life**: Embrace the cross and find God in it 32

II. More Power

4. More Power Through the Charisms 37
    A. **Love**: Releases the charisms 37
    B. **Power**: Charisms and service 39
    C. **Wisdom**: Charisms and maturity 41

5. More Power Through Community 43
    A. **Accept** the call to community 43
    B. **Build** committed relationships 45
    C. **Heal** broken relationships 47

6. More Power Through Service 51
    A. **Called** to zeal 52
    B. **Gifted** with the Spirit 53
    C. **Sent** to be effectively evangelistic 54

III. More Wisdom

7. More Wisdom Through Discernment 61
    A. **Listening**: Attitudes we need to hear God's will 61
    B. **Knowing**: Objective criteria for testing the Spirit 63
    C. **Hearing**: Subjective criteria for testing inspirations of the Spirit 65
    D. The Charismatic **Gift** of Discernment 67
    E. **Waiting** on the Lord 67

8. More Wisdom Through Vision 69
    A. **Developing** a common vision 69
    B. The **Vision** of the Catholic Charismatic Renewal in the Church and the world 70
    C. The **Mission** of the Catholic Charismatic Renewal in the Church and the world 73
    D. Some **Challenges** to the Catholic Charismatic Renewal 74

9. More Wisdom Through Hope 77
    A. The **Spirit** leads us to hope 77
    B. **Hope** deepens life in the Spirit 79
    C. **Patience** brings us to the promise of the Spirit we hope for 81

Discussion Starters for Sharing Groups 83

Questions for Personal Reflection 89

Growth Seminar Additional Resources 103

Foreword

For a number of years the National Service Committee has had discussions about developing a Growth Seminar for those who had recently been brought into a personal relationship with Jesus Christ and a renewed life in the Spirit through Holy Spirit Seminars held in prayer groups and parishes, as well as for those in the Catholic Charismatic Renewal who might need refreshment.

At the same time, Sr. Nancy Kellar, S.C., after her service as Director of the International Catholic Charismatic Renewal Services office in Rome, had felt the Lord calling her to put on paper a number of the talks that she had developed over the years. A conversation between Sr. Nancy and myself resulted in a proposal that led to the National Service Committee publishing this nine-week Growth Seminar: *There's Always More: Expecting New Fire*.

The Seminar is designed to be given in group settings, such as during prayer meetings or a Retreat Day. Each talk is presented in extended outline form and the book includes an introductory "Preparation for Teachers" and "Discussion Starters for Sharing Groups." The book may also be used by individuals for their own personal spiritual growth.

It is the hope of the National Service Committee that use of this book will strengthen all those who use it: those who give the talks, those who hear the talks, as well as prayer groups and the Catholic Charismatic Renewal as a whole.

Let us know how it works for you.

Walter Matthews
Executive Director
National Service Committee

Preparation For Teachers

Some time ago there was a drama contest in England for which there was a significant money prize. The contestants were asked to read Psalm 23, the psalm of the Good Shepherd. A well-known Shakespearean actor entered the contest, as well as a poor farmer who needed the money to save his farm.

The actor read the psalm with great drama and feeling, and received generous applause for his effort.

As the farmer approached the stage, the actor scoffed, "Who does he think he is competing against me?" As the farmer read the psalm people began to cry. The actor mocked, "It is so bad they are crying!" When the farmer finished there was dead silence. The actor thought, "Wouldn't you think at least one person would acknowledge the farmer for his effort?"

After the silence, the crowd stood and gave the farmer thunderous applause! The farmer won the contest.

Afterward, because of the protests of the actor, the judges said to him, "You knew the psalm, but the poor farmer knew the Shepherd."

Key Point
The teacher is a shepherd of people and the most important thing is for him or her to know the Shepherd.

"Whoever is called 'to teach Christ' must first seek 'the surpassing worth of knowing Christ Jesus.' …From this loving knowledge of Christ springs the desire to proclaim him" (*Catechism of the Catholic Church*, 428-429. Hereafter referred to as *CCC*, followed by the section number.)

I. Why teaching?
The importance of teaching might seem obvious, but some still say, "Why do we need teaching?"

We need to be convinced that short teachings in our prayer meetings and community gatherings are a part of the way God wants us to continue to bring people to know Jesus and to help them grow in the Spirit.

A. It is the will of the Father. In Hosea God chastised the priests of Israel because they were ignoring their responsibility to teach.
- "My people perish for want of knowledge. Since you yourself have rejected knowledge, so I shall reject you from my priesthood; since you have for-

gotten the teaching of your God, I in my turn shall forget your children" (Ho 4:6).

B. Jesus wants His people to be taught. He sent out the apostles with the threefold command to preach, to teach and to heal.
- "He sent them out to proclaim the kingdom of God and to heal" (Lk 9:2).
- Jesus made it the way He expects us to show our love for Him. "'Do you love me? ... Feed my lambs ... Look after my sheep ... Feed my sheep'" (Jn 21:15-17).

C. The gift of teaching is one of the gifts listed among the charisms.
- "And to some, his 'gift' was that they should be apostles; to some prophets; to some, evangelists; to some, pastors and teachers; to knit God's holy people together for the work of service to build up the Body of Christ" (Eph 4:11-12).
- "Then since the gifts that we have differ according to the grace that was given to each of us ... let us devote ourselves ... if it is teaching, to teaching" (Rom 12:6-7).

II. What is the goal of teaching?
Only if teachers know what their goals look like will they have the objective criteria against which to evaluate the results of their efforts.

The goal of Christian teaching is to bring every person to greater maturity in Christ and in Christian living.
- "It is Christ among you, your hope of glory: this is the Christ we are proclaiming, admonishing and instructing everyone in all wisdom, to make everyone perfect in Christ" (Col 1:27-28).

A. Christian initiation
1. The **primary goal** of Christian initiation is to bring people into a new way of life.
- Those who teach and pray with people to help them come into the Christian life must be able to tell whether a conversion of life has taken place in the people they are working with. Unless we know how to help someone to make the necessary initial changes in their life, we will not be able to assess their progress and move them on to growth teaching.

2. The **secondary goal** of Christian initiation is to connect people with a group of Christians.
- It is not enough to bring people to an isolated moment of Christian commitment. We must bring them to an enduring Christian way of life.
- To test the effectiveness of an initiation process, one has only to ask:
  - Are lives changing?
  - Are those who have gone through the initiation program—The Life in the Spirit Seminar or another initiation series—joining a body of people living the Christian life?

B. Growth teaching
1. The **primary goal** of growth teaching is to strengthen the foundation of Christian maturity. It is to help individuals to understand, appropriate and grow in the Christian life by teaching them how:
- To yield to the Spirit, to pray, to deal with suffering, to know God's will, and to move on in the Spirit.

2. The **secondary goal** is to fortify the Christian's relationships by helping individuals:
- To recognize and be free of wrongdoing, to learn to relate better in the family and the Christian community, and to accept the call to build committed relationships and to reconcile broken relationships.

3. The **third goal** is to motivate and empower the Christian for service by equipping them with spiritual gifts, with vision and zeal for service and with practical knowledge of how to serve.

This seminar is an example of growth teaching. It is different than teaching about Catholic/Christian doctrine and dogma that requires study in fields like theology, morality and Church history.

III. Who should teach?
In the Church there is a close link between teaching and pastoring. The Pope and Bishops are both pastors and teachers for the Church. In prayer groups and communities there is often a similar connection.

A. **Those who have the overall responsibility** for the group are often also given the gift of teaching.
- That is not to say that all leaders have teaching gifts or have them in the same degree.
- Nor is it to say that only leaders should teach, but there is often a link between the two.

B. **Those who have the charism for teaching.**
- The gift of teaching is a charism for making Christian truth clear, life-giving and attractive. There are different gifts for different kinds of teaching.
- Some are gifted to give exhortative teaching that calls the community again and again to live the basic Gospel message.
- Others have the gift of informative teaching that helps the community develop new understanding of the Christian life.
- The ideal is for a balance of both of these so that the variety of the different gifts may be used for the up-building of the community.

C. **A sense of his or her own unworthiness is helpful for one who teaches.**
"'I am a man of unclean lips' … then one of the seraphs … touched my mouth … 'your guilt has been removed' … 'Whom shall I send?' … 'Here am I, send me'" (Is 6:5-8).
- A sense of sinfulness calls individuals to a reverential humility, to a fear of the Lord realizing that they are handling the sacred when they handle the Word of God.
- It requires such reverence so that the teacher uses the time with responsibility, not using the time to "grind an ax," to give pet peeves or pet opinions.
- A sense of inadequacy leads us to rely on God's power and not our own.

D. **A teacher is willing to be purified.**
If God wants us to minister in any way He is going to see to it that we are purified, that we are pruned.
- A key to becoming a good teacher is that we submit to purification. "Only a few of you … should be teachers, bearing in mind that we shall receive a stricter judgement" (Jas 3:1). Teachers will be called to account by their own words and also by the words of others. God sent an angel to Isaiah; but to us He sends our neighbor.
- Giving correction. Most of us recoil at the suggestion that our work for the Lord and His people ought to be regularly evaluated, but good order and ef-

fective service are impossible without regular evaluations. In fact, evaluation can be liberating and upbuilding when undertaken in love and commitment.
- Encouragement is one of the primary purposes for evaluation. The branches that are producing fruit are pruned to produce more. Leaders who are pruning each other's gifts need to learn to commend people for what they have done well. Often an entire evaluation might consist in exchanging ideas for improving what was basically done well.
- When pointing out problems the more specific, concise and objective the better. Avoid hinting, or beating around the bush, in the hope that people will get the point without our trying to make it. Evasion is not kindness. It is devious and manipulative. In the name of love we avoid making constructive criticism, but real love seeks what is best for the other.

> My son do not scorn correction from the Lord, do not resent his training, for the Lord trains those he loves, and chastises every son he accepts (Heb 12:5-6).

E. Teachers are people who are willing to respond generously to God's call to serve.
- Willing to respond, "Here am I, send me" (Is 6:8).
- Moves from seeing service as something I have to do, to something I am privileged to do. "I, who am less than the least of all God's holy people, have been entrusted with this special grace" (Eph 3:8).
- Convinced that we will grow as we serve.

F. Teachers are willing to persevere without seeing results or getting credit for the effort.
- "Proclaim the message and, welcome or unwelcome, insist on it … but do all with patience …" (2 Tim 4:2). "'Until when, Lord?' … 'Until towns are in ruins and deserted'" (Is 6:11).

IV. How to teach? The elements of a good teaching
Learning to give a teaching is like learning to cook. You need the right **ingredients, the right seasoning, the right blend, and the right timing.**

A. The right ingredients: The ingredients are the basic contents of a teaching.
- They are the information, knowledge, truth, understanding, and insight that the person who is teaching aims to impart.

- They may come from personal reflection on the teachings of Jesus in Scripture, the teaching of the Church from the writings of Church Fathers and the Popes, the truths passed on to us in the traditions of the Church, our everyday experiences in the world or from the suggested content of a seminar outline.

B. The right seasoning: These are the stories and personal experiences that explain or clarify, that is, add spice to the basic ingredients.
- The more clearly the truth is presented, not too theoretical but practical, the more people can take it in and use it. The information sets a context for the practical down-to-earth advice we really want to communicate.
- The more people can identify with the truth as presented, the more people can say, "I know just what you mean; that is just the kind of thing that happens to me." When we reach people at that level they will be able to receive and apply the teaching we give them more thoroughly.

C. The right blend: A good teaching blends inspiration with information. It needs to touch the heart as well as open the mind.
- Teachers need to be touched in their own spirit by the anointing of the Holy Spirit if their words are to motivate and draw others toward the truth they are communicating.
- Inspiration does not equal emotion. It may involve emotion, but it goes deeper than emotions that are on the surface of our lives. If inspiration only appeals to the emotions it does not go deep enough.

D. The right timing: One of the most difficult things to achieve in a good teaching is the right timing. If it is too short the information will not have enough clarification. If it is too long it will not keep the attention of the people.
- It helps to start with a story to get people's attention and to end with questions that lead them to make concrete applications of the information and with prayer that gives them time to respond to the inspiration.

V. Preparation for the teachers of this Growth Seminar

The seminar requires preparation on the part of both the team of people who will work together during the nine weeks and the individuals who will give the various talks of each session.

A. How does the team of teachers prepare?
1. Study the "Preparation for Teachers."
The team preparing to give the Growth Seminar would do well to give themselves a teaching session using points I to IV of this "Preparation For Teachers" on the Why? What? Who? How? of teaching.
- This session will help teachers recognize their own gifts and the type of teaching for which they are most gifted.

2. Become familiar with the presentation format and content.
Review the format and be clear about the goals of each session.
- Become familiar enough with the content of each seminar session to discern which member of the team has the knowledge and the experience to teach which session.

3. Pray together before each seminar session.
The team prays together so that their confidence is not in their ability but in the power of God anointing them.
- Listen together for the fresh Word of God for their particular group on that particular night. Pray over and encourage the teacher for that night.

4. Review the previous session.
At some point before the beginning of the following session review the previous session. Review the entire night, from beginning to end, and not just the talk that was given.
- Were the people warmly welcomed? Were they given a chance to connect with those whom they knew from the Life in the Spirit Seminar?
- Did the time of praise and worship prepare them to listen with their whole being to the Word of God?
- How clearly was the content of the teaching presented? Was there enough personal witness to keep people's attention? Was the timing just right or was it too long or too short? Did it achieve the session goals?
- What was the experience of the discussion groups? Was the leadership of the groups effective? Did everyone get a chance to speak?
- Are there any changes that need to be made to improve any part of the Seminar session?

B. How does an individual teacher prepare?
1. Be faithful to personal prayer.
The only way to know the Shepherd is by being faithful to daily personal prayer. Pray through and apply to one's life the second session, "More Love Through Prayer."

2. Absorb the presentation content.
Become so familiar with the suggested content of the teaching session that it becomes one's own.

3. Search one's heart for personal experiences.
Each session of the seminar has a suggested story or image as a starting point to introduce the theme of the content. However, the personal experiences that are the spice of the session must come from the presenter's own life.

4. Answer the "questions for discussion."
Each session has questions for the participants to discuss. (See the section "Discussion Starters for Sharing Groups," page 83.) The presenters need to answer those questions for themselves out of their own experiences. This will help them become more convinced of the importance of the material they are going to communicate. (Note: A limited number of copies of the Discussion Starters may be made for each session.)

5. Browse suggested resources.
Each seminar session has a list of resource books and video tapes. (See the section "Growth Seminar Additional Resources," page 103.) Browse these for additional material to enhance the suggested content of each seminar session. Become familiar enough with them so that one can make recommendations to seminar participants.

VI. Suggested format for the seminar night

The teaching content of this Growth Seminar has three distinct units and each unit has three sessions. The nine sessions can be presented in nine consecutive weeks, as the Life in the Spirit Seminar is done in seven weeks.

It might also be done three weeks at a time by treating each unit as a distinct seminar. The material in each session is full enough that a session might be done in two weeks thus extending a unit to five or six weeks.

Session I is shorter than the others to allow time for various introductory remarks by presenters.

If the seminar does not follow soon after a Life in the Spirit Seminar, the presenters should review the suggestions for the team presented in Part I, A to C of *The New Life in the Spirit Seminars Team Manual: Catholic Edition 2000*.

In the introductory remarks for Session I review with the participants Part I (E) of *The New Life in the Spirit Seminars Team Manual* on the importance of continuing "Community Building" during the Growth Seminar.

A possible timeline for each seminar session might be:

15 minutes	Prayer and Praise
30 minutes	Teaching
20-30 minutes	Sharing groups followed by intercessory prayer
15-30 minutes	Closing social

If the team decides to cover the material in some sessions in two weeks instead of one they might do the teaching in 20 minutes and lengthen the sharing time.

This seminar could be given as a series of one-day retreats. In a full-day retreat you could allow more time for Prayer and Praise, and personal prayer ministry among the participants. There is enough material in each unit, for example, "More Love" with its three sessions, to fill a day retreat. It would be unwise to try to do all nine sessions in a single day.

Some prayer groups might decide to present this seminar as part of their prayer meetings. In that case, a 10-15 minute teaching is recommended. You will notice that all but two sessions have three parts. A single part would provide enough material for a prayer meeting teaching. For example, "A. Desire: More of the promises for personal renewal" in the session, "Expecting More of the Fire of the Holy Spirit," could be one teaching.

Conclusion

Good teachers are Christ's gift through the power of the Spirit. Let's expect that the Lord will provide them. If your prayer group or community does not have them, ask the Lord to give them. Ask the Lord to continually improve the teachers that the prayer group or community does have now.

Unit I

More Love

Fan into flame…the Spirit of…love (2 Tim 1:6-7).

Session 1
Expecting More of the Fire of the Holy Spirit

*"Have I not told you that if you believe
you will see the glory of God?" (Jn 11:40).*

Goals
1. To lead people to see baptism in the Holy Spirit as an ongoing experience.
2. To reveal the obstacles to further surrendering to the Spirit.

Framing Image
In Uganda a group of young people acted out the message of seeking more of the Spirit.

One youngster held a large pitcher of water, representing the Spirit, ready to fill the containers of anyone who asked for more.

One young girl came carrying a small thimble and crying, "Fill me, Lord!" Her container was so small she could only receive a few drops.

A young man with a slightly larger container, filled with many things cried, "Fill me, Lord!" His container could receive nothing more because it was already filled.

Still another young person came with a really large container. It looked very hopeful as he cried, "Fill me, Lord!" However, as the water was poured into his container it ran out the bottom because the container had holes!

Finally, a group of youngsters came forward with a large, empty container. It was able to be filled to capacity with the water representing the Spirit. Rejoicing they took the water, and gave it to everyone gathered so that it could be filled again and again!

Key Point
Being baptized in the Holy Spirit is an ongoing experience of Pentecost. It is a release of the Holy Spirit such that we experience all that God promises us as our inheritance. It is an ongoing experience in which there is always more that we can receive.

A. Desire: More of the promises for personal renewal.
1. We can lose the fire of the Spirit if we lose our expectancy. "'Have I not told you that if you believe you will see the glory of God.'" (Jn 11:40).

In John 11, Jesus was calling Martha and Mary to expectant faith.
a. Expectant faith is not new efforts. It is new desire.
- Growing in expectant faith is growing in desire. The more we desire, the more we ask for. The more we ask for, the more we receive.

b. Do we continue to expect more of the Spirit?
- We were renewed in the Spirit because we were led to expect more of the power of the Spirit. We need to keep that expectancy.
- Like the prophet in Ezekiel 47 we are being invited to go deeper and deeper into the stream of the Spirit.

2. We can lose the fire of the Spirit if we limit our expectancy.
"Be filled with the Spirit" (Eph 5:18). The verb is an active participle indicating an ongoing filling.

a. We need to desire a deepening of the basic promise of the Spirit for personal renewal.
- There is always more of the Holy Spirit to receive in the promises:
"'They will all know me, from least to greatest'" (Jer 31:34).
"So that we may understand the lavish gifts God has given us" (1 Cor 2:12).

b. Do we expect the fullness of the promises of the Holy Spirit?
- There is always more to yield to the Holy Spirit in the promises:
"One person will say, 'I belong to Yahweh'" (Is 44:5),
It is only in the Holy Spirit that we can say "Jesus is Lord" (1 Cor 12:3), and "*Abba*, Father" (Gal 4:6).

B. Detachment: Be emptied of the obstacles to growth.

1. Experiencing the ongoing release of the Spirit means ongoing repentance and ongoing surrender to Jesus as Lord of our lives.

When the crowd saw the Spirit alive in the apostles at Pentecost they asked, "'What are we to do, brothers?' 'You must repent,' Peter answered, 'and every one of you must be baptized in the name of Jesus Christ…and you will receive the gift of the Holy Spirit'" (Acts 2:37-38).

a. We can't separate receiving more through ongoing expectant faith from being emptied again and again in ongoing repentance.
- Walking in the Spirit does not mean that we will never fall again. Such false expectation after finding new life in the Spirit can lead to discouragement.

b. It is repentance, not remorse, which God asks for.
- Sin is falling short of the mark and repentance is refocusing, turning around again toward the Lord. It is what St. Peter did and it leads to new life in the Spirit and holiness.

- Remorse is seeing our sin and turning in on ourselves. That is what Judas did and it leads to death.

c. Ongoing repentance leads to holiness.
- When we live in an attitude of ongoing repentance the time between our sin and our repentance grows shorter and shorter until repentance comes against temptation and aborts the sin.

2. We need to be emptied again in ongoing surrender to Jesus as Lord of our lives. The Lord can only fill the empty. Are we expecting God to fill a container that is already filled?

In the parable of the seed Jesus reminds us that the seed, even after it is received into the ground with joy, can be choked by the **worries, the riches, the pleasures** of life (see Mk 4:19). We need to be emptied again of all the burdens, fears, and anxieties we take on.

a. Worries
- We can take on all the **old worries** again, worries for our family, worries for our finances.
- We can take on **new worries**, worries about our spiritual lives, worries for our prayer groups until we have more worries now than we had before.
- Remember what we heard in the beginning of our life in the Spirit,
    Unless the LORD build the house,
    they labor in vain who build it (Ps 127:1) (NAB).

b. Riches
- We can seek after all the **old riches** again in material goods.
- We can seek the **new riches** of spiritual gifts and spiritual experiences in such a way that we lose sight of the Giver of all good gifts.

c. Pleasures
- We can long for all the old **pleasures** again and **new pleasures**.
- We can look for the pleasure of acceptance so that we stifle the new life in the Spirit and the gifts of the Spirit because it is unpopular to look too Christian or too charismatic.

C. Dependence: Surrender anew to the release of the Spirit.
Are we stifling the fire of the Spirit by beginning to take control of our lives again?

1. Trust releases the power of God to act in us.

"'Blessed is she who believed that the promise made her by the Lord would be fulfilled'" (Lk 1:45).

a. Expectant faith is trusting faith.
- The expectant faith that released the fire of the Spirit to act in Mary was more than believing faith, it was trusting faith.

b. Trust moves beyond believing in our heads that God is faithful to His promises.
- Trust means abandonment of our lives to God with confidence in His faithfulness. Trapeze artists must trust that their partners are going to catch them when they let go, swinging in the air to their outstretched hands.

2. To grow in the Spirit we need to grow in this kind of radical trust in the faithfulness of God to His promises.

In Acts 26, when Paul was given the opportunity to defend himself, he could have said, "I raised the dead, I healed the sick, I survived a shipwreck, and I broke down prison walls." He said simply, "'It is for my hope in the promise made by God…that I am on trial'" (Acts 26:6).
- Paul knew that the source of all the power in his life and ministry came from his dependence on God's power.
- To grow in the Spirit we need to grow in this kind of radical trust in the faithfulness of God to His promises.

3. The enemy of the deeper dependence that is key to growth in the Spirit is fear.

The Lord understood that we would fear surrender. He assured us, "'What father among you, if his son asked for a fish, would hand him a snake? …How much more will our heavenly Father give the Holy Spirit to those who ask him!'" (Lk 11:11-13).

Fear paralyzes and closes us to the more God has for us.
- **Fear of God,** of what He might ask of us, is a lack of confidence that He can satisfy all our desires. "Make Yahweh your only joy and he will give you your heart's desires" (Ps 37:4).
- **Fear of ourselves,** of our inadequacy is often a false humility. We need to remember that everything is gift.

Are we offering God a container filled with holes, weakened because we have begun to rely on our power again?

Are we stifling the fire of the Spirit by beginning to rely on ourselves again?

Session 2
More Love Through Prayer

"You did not choose me, no, I chose you" (Jn 15:16).

Goals
1. To come to a deeper knowledge of God's love through growth in prayer.
2. To recognize and overcome difficulties in prayer.

Framing Story
A little boy stood by the side of a railroad track waving a little red flag. A curious onlooker inquired why he was doing that. The little boy answered that the big locomotive train stopped when he waved his little red flag. The onlooker discouraged him saying, "No, it wouldn't stop because there was no station"; but the little boy persisted. As the train approached it slowed down and came to a stop while the motorman reached down, picked up the little boy, and drew him to his lap. The onlooker stood gazing in amazement when the boy pointed to the motorman and called out the window, "He's my Daddy."

Key Point
Prayer is allowing God to reach down and draw us to Himself. It is God's initiative of love planted in the heart of every human being in his or her mother's womb. St. Augustine said, "You have made us for yourself, O Lord, and our hearts are restless until they rest in you."

A. Be *Available* to the Father's recreating love.
1. God's love is personal and we need to be available.
"'Before I formed you in the womb I knew you; before you came to birth I consecrated you'" (Jer 1:5).
a. Believe He calls each of us by name.
"'I am the good shepherd; I know my own, and my own know me'" (Jn 10:14).
b. Surrender to the power of that call to change us, to heal us.
- The apostles left everything when they heard Him call their name (see Mt 4:18-22).
- Lazarus came out of the tomb when Jesus called his name (see Jn 11:40-44).
- Mary recognized Him at the tomb when she heard Him call her name (see Jn 20:16).

2. Obstacles to the experience of being personally loved in prayer
a. Failure to be still
Paul prays for "strength to grasp the breadth and the length, the height and depth … [of] the love of Christ" (Eph 3:17-18).
- Why does Paul pray for strength to grasp God's love? It takes strength to be still, to stop running, even doing good things for God.
- It is the strength St. Peter needed at the Last Supper when Jesus bent to wash his feet. Peter was ready to do anything for Jesus at that moment. However, Jesus asked him simply to be still and let himself be loved. Peter protested because it takes strength to be still to let the Lord Jesus love us.

b. Failure to expect Him to call us by name
"She had heard about Jesus, and she came up through the crowd and touched his cloak" (Mk 5:27).

The woman with the hemorrhage was content to stay in the crowd, to simply touch the hem of Jesus' garment. He was on the way to the house of an important official of the synagogue. She believed He could heal her; but she did not think she was important enough for Him to stop just for her.
- We can be like that woman saying, "I believe He loves US, but I don't believe I'm important enough for him to love ME, so I'll take a little bit left over from all those really good people or important people that He loves."
- As He did for that woman, Jesus calls us out of the crowd. He calls us each by name and pours out His healing love on us.

3. Being available also means taking time for prayer.
"Mary brought in a pound of very costly ointment, pure nard, and with it anointed the feet of Jesus" (Jn 12:3). Jesus praised the generosity of Mary for giving her best ointment.

In human relationships, if we expect them to grow into friendships, we need to move from spontaneous, periodic meetings to appointments and regular communication. The same is true in developing our relationship with God in prayer.

a. Prime time. As we look for a likely time to pray, we ought to bear in mind that the best time, not left over time, belongs to the Lord.
- Emergencies do arise that can cancel our prayer time. We can compensate for those times by having a "back up time" later in the day.

b. The right time. How much time should we reserve for prayer? When we are new to prayer, it is better to select a short time, perhaps 15 or 20 minutes.

- Then as we learn to pray and feel more comfortable praying, we can extend the period until we reach a length that's right for us. The most important point is to choose a reasonable length of time and stick to it.

c. **The right place.** A place where we can have some privacy and won't be interrupted is desirable, sometimes essential.
- A family man with 13 children was sure there was no quiet place for prayer in his house. The Lord showed him a place behind the furnace that the children didn't know about!

"All who are guided by the Spirit of God are sons of God" (Rom 8:15).

Are we taking time for prayer and allowing ourselves to hear him say, "You are my beloved daughter, you are my beloved son?"

B. Be *Vulnerable* to Jesus' healing love.

1. God's love is unconditional and we need to be vulnerable.

"While he was still a long way off, his father saw him and…ran to the boy" (Lk 15:20). The story of the prodigal son (see Lk 15:11-32) is Jesus' revelation of the Father's unconditional love for us. The Father's love is a free gift that we can't earn, that we don't deserve, that doesn't diminish with our unfaithfulness.

a. Scripture has been called God's love story of wooing and pursuing His people.
- In Hosea God gives us the image of the faithful husband going after his unfaithful wife again and again.
- In Isaiah 49 God uses the image of a mother's love, "Can a woman forget her baby at the breast, feel no pity for the child she has borne? Even if these were to forget, I shall not forget you" (Is 49:15).

b. Jesus is so anxious for us to believe the Father's unconditional love He gives us many images.
- From nature—the image of the mother hen who gathers her chicks under her wings (see Mt 23:37), of the shepherd who goes after the lost sheep (see Lk 15:4-6).
- From life—the lost coin (see Lk 15:8-9) and the treasure hidden in the field (see Mt 13:44).

c. Ultimately Jesus gives His own life to reveal the Father's unconditional love.
"You could hardly find anyone ready to die even for someone upright; though it is just possible that, for a really good person, someone might undertake to die" (Rom 5:7).

2. Obstacles to knowing more deeply his unconditional love through prayer
"This people's heart is torpid, their ears dulled, they have shut their eyes tight, to avoid using their eyes to see, their ears to hear, using their heart to understand, changing their ways and being healed by me" (Acts 28:27).
a. We have a pagan image of God as the avenging judge.
- We make God's love like our own. Our capacity for faithfulness is so limited; we presume God's love is like ours.

b. We experience our sin and say God couldn't love me anymore.
- We put ourselves under condemnation. We refuse God's life-changing mercy.

c. We want to avoid painful questions. If we allow God to get too close, will we have to change?
- We can be like the woman at the well who changed the subject when Jesus began to reveal He knew her life and sins (see Jn 4:20).

3. Being vulnerable in prayer is being real before Him with no masks.
"Now Martha, who was distracted with all the serving, came to him and said, 'Lord, do you not care that my sister is leaving me to do the serving all by myself? Please tell her to help me'" (Lk 10:40).

Martha, Mary and Lazarus acknowledged Jesus as Lord, but their friendship was intimate enough to involve Him in their family argument!

God meets us where we are, so we need to be where we are, or we won't meet God:

a. with our sin, neither condemning nor acquitting ourselves (see 1 Cor 4: 3-5).

b. with our troubles, even when they seem so insignificant, we persuade ourselves that God's love does not extend to this or that facet of our lives.
- "I pour out my worry in his presence, in his presence I unfold my troubles" (Ps 142:2).

c. with our distractions and make them our prayer because that is where God will meet us.

d. with our sickness and be sick with Him. A parent is most attentive to the child that is sick.

"Jesus said, 'This sickness will not end in death, but it is for God's glory so that through it the Son of God may be glorified'" (Jn 11:4).

Are we being vulnerable with God in prayer or are we hiding our real selves from Him?

C. Be *Expectant* of the Spirit's sanctifying love.
1. God's love is everlasting and unlimited and we need to be expectant.
"For this is how God loved the world: he gave his only Son, so that everyone who believes in him may not perish but may have eternal life" (Jn 3:16).

The Father gives his Son and the Son gives His own life to reveal the Father's unlimited love.
- Any act of our infinite God could have saved us. But, He chose the ignominious death on the cross because He knew what speaks to us most of one person's love for another is that he/she would lay down his/her life for another.
- The Church has raised up to sainthood Maxmilian Kolbe because he made the sacrifice of his life for another.

2. Trials can be obstacles to our knowing God's unlimited love in prayer
"Can anything cut us off from the love of Christ-can hardships or distress, or persecution, or lack of food and clothing, or threats or violence?" (Rom 8:35).

In His unlimited love God is always turned towards us even when we don't experience it. However, we can let trouble separate us from God. We say, "How could a loving God let this happen?"
- In her book *The Hiding Place* Corrie Ten Boom tells the story of her family who was imprisoned for helping Jews during WWII. They were able to hide a small New Testament in their barracks in the concentration camp. They tried to read the Word to the other inmates but it was too difficult because the guards kept coming in and out. Then the barracks became infested with lice. Their first reaction was, "God, what more can happen!" Then they realized the blessing of the lice. The guards no longer came into the barracks and it became a house of prayer preparing people for their deaths. Corrie's sister, who died in the camp said, "Tell the world there is no pit so deep that his love is not deeper still."
- Jesus never promised there would be no wilderness. He promised to be a path in the wilderness.

3. Being expectantly open to the Spirit in prayer means including specific elements in our prayer.
a. **Worship,** spontaneous praise in the name of Jesus, praise in song, praise with the charismatic gift of tongues, lifts our hearts up to God.
- "Let us go into his dwelling-place, and worship at his footstool" (Ps 132:7).

b. **Reading Scripture** with the readings of the day's liturgy, spontaneous opening to Scripture, or using a Scripture guide to prayer can help raise our minds to God.
- We need to listen to the Word asking, "Lord, what are You saying?"
- "What are You saying to me?" Let the Word move us to love for the Lord, to root out sin, and to overcome the obstacles in us to a deeper prayer life.

c. **Intercession,** as we end our prayer, focuses us outward in service to the Church and the world.
- "I urge then, first of all that petitions, prayers, intercessions and thanksgiving should be offered for everyone" (1 Tim 2:1).

Are we willing to come with expectant faith to let Him set us free of these obstacles to knowing his unconditional love?

Summary:
The attitudes needed to grow in love through prayer are the attitudes of Mary. Her AVE was:

> She was **Available**—waiting in prayer to hear Word of God (see Lk 1:28).
>
> She was **Vulnerable**—she asked the question in her mind "'But how can this come about, since I have no knowledge of man?'" (Lk 1:34).
>
> She was **Expectant**—"'Blessed is she who believed that the promise made her by the Lord would be fulfilled'" (Lk 1:45).

Session 3
More Love Through Purification

Even were I to walk in a ravine as dark as death I should fear no danger, for you are at my side (Ps 23:4).

Goals
1. To learn how to grow through suffering.
2. To recognize purification as a normal part of spiritual growth.

Framing Image
In the world of shepherding, the shepherd must find new ranges for his flock after the "home" period of the winter. In the summer months he takes them to the highlands. This often entails long "drives." This is done in the midst of the danger of sudden storms, wild animals, rockslides, and avalanches. But there is no other way to reach the rich pastures of the highlands. The valley is the only road. During this time the flock is entirely alone with the shepherd. They are in intimate contact with him and under his most watchful attention day and night.

Key Point
In the Christian life we often speak of wanting "to move to higher ground with God." We want to move beyond the common ground and move to a more intimate walk with God. We speak of mountaintop experiences and we envy those who have ascended the heights and entered into this more sublime sort of life. It is as though we imagined we could be "air lifted "to higher ground. In the Christian life this is not so.
- **As with sheep management, so with God's people, one only gains higher ground by climbing through the valleys.**

A. The Truth: Recognize and overcome misconceptions.
Some misconceptions about suffering must be overcome before our valleys, our suffering, can be a place where we encounter God.

1. First, the misconception that all suffering is "darkness" and therefore God cannot be found in it.

a. There seems to be an apparent contradiction in Scripture unless we understand the Light - Darkness theme.

- In Ps 23:4 we hear, "Even were I to walk in a ravine as dark as death I should fear no danger."
- In John, Jesus says, "'Anyone who follows me will not be walking in the dark'" (8:12).
- Is there a conflict here? Not if we understand that we can walk through the "valley of darkness" in the light, if the very darkness leads us to God!

b. The truth is that "light" is anything that shows us the way to God, and that can include suffering.
- The Psalm says, "Even were I to walk in a ravine as dark as death." It does not say I die there, or stop there, but rather "I walk in."
- The words of Ps 139:12 have new meaning: "Even darkness to you is not dark, and night is clear as the day."

Any shepherd familiar with the high country knows that the best route to the top is along these dark valleys. He leads his flocks gently but persistently up the paths that wind through them.

2. Second, the misconception that the only time we meet God in suffering is when we are healed.

a. We can fail to be "with God" in our moments of suffering because we fail to recognize His presence in our cross.
- In the past we didn't pray for healing because we thought it was better to suffer than to ask to be healed. Now we often assume that a failure to be healed must mean we are doing something wrong. We assume we don't have enough faith or the person praying with us doesn't have enough faith or we haven't found the right formula for praying.

b. The truth is that healing does not replace the cross. Jesus never promised that there would not be a cross. He promised that He would carry the cross with us.
- Jesus as our Good Shepherd has done the same. He has gone before us with the cross and He invites us to follow Him, to walk in His footsteps.
- Our God is not limited to what we see as good and beautiful. He chose the excruciating and shameful death of a criminal and made it the way to the Resurrection.

The shepherd never took his flock where he had not already been before. He was familiar with all the dangers and was fully prepared to safeguard his flock under every circumstance

B. The Way: Acknowledge and accept that purification leads to maturity.
1. Realize that purification is a normal part of spiritual growth.
Jesus was led by the Spirit through the wilderness, being tempted there by the devil for forty days. Then Jesus was filled with the Holy Spirit and went to Galilee to preach (see Lk 4:1-14).
a. The Spirit is only fully released in us when we, like Jesus, confront the desert in our lives and persevere through it.
- Persevering through suffering in our life in the physical, emotional and psychological problems in ourselves and those we love is responding as Jesus did when He said, "'Human beings live not on bread alone'" (Lk 4:4).
- Persevering through the suffering that comes from trying to live the Christian life, facing misunderstanding, criticism, even persecution is following Jesus who said, "'You must do homage to the Lord your God, him alone you must serve'" (Lk 4:8).
- Persevering through the suffering that comes from not being able to bring our families, especially our teens and our elderly, to follow Jesus is sharing the powerlessness of Jesus who resisted the temptation to ask the Father to show His power over the universe. "'Do not put the Lord your God to the test'" (Lk 4:12).

2. Recognize the maturing process and grow in the Spirit through it.
Our weakening in the life in the Spirit can simply be a failure to recognize that our charismatic spiritual maturing will go through the same "testing by fire" that the great spiritual masters have told us about down through the ages.
a. God often withdraws the initial fervor. He sustains us by a hidden power that does not have such manifest experiences.
b. One of the effects of being baptized in the Holy Spirit is a new and felt relationship with the Lord.
- God is very close and prayer is a joy. People feel elated and enthusiastic for the things of the Spirit. There are good days and bad, but generally we can explain these by our fidelity and infidelity.
- After a while, even while being faithful to our prayer time, the enthusiasm passes, the good feelings fade and prayer becomes less satisfying.

c. This normal and common experience can discourage people.
- They fail to recognize that God purifies us of whatever attachments would keep us from closer union with Him, not only sin, but attachments to our good feelings that can lead us to think we are holier than we are.

3. Allow the Lord to teach us through suffering.

God purifies us so that we learn that:

a. Love, not exuberance, is the essence of the spiritual life (see Mt 7:12).

b. Faith, not spiritual experience, is the foundation of the spiritual life (see Heb 11).

c. Humility, not spiritual power, is the shield that protects our Christian life (see 2 Cor 12:8-9).

d. Perseverance under trials of all sorts is the test that proves, deepens and confirms the Christian life (see Rom 5:3–4). If we learn this lesson through purification, He will renew our exuberance, give us new spiritual power and new spiritual experiences.

C. The Life: Embrace the cross and find God in it.

1. We can resist purification and become bitter, or submit to it and become holy!

"It makes me happy to be suffering for you now, and in my own body to make up all the hardships that still have to be undergone by Christ for the sake of his body, the Church" (Col 1:24).

a. God comes to us and loves us and reveals Himself to us just as we are. For most of us that includes periods of suffering.

b. If suffering is part of the way we are right now, then suffering is part of the way the Lord is touching us.

- If God is touching us through the suffering then even the suffering is to be embraced, not because in some perverse way we enjoy pain but simply because He is there.

c. We embrace it in order to find Him, and to hear what He is telling us about Himself, and about ourselves.

2. Purification comes in our spiritual lives.

Dryness, a sense of the absence of God in prayer, can be a suffering that means growth if it increases our desire for God. It is a peaceful desire that is secure in darkness, knowing that the sense of the absence of God is an illusion.

a. Prayer is moving away from the illusion that God is absent toward the conviction that God is present, even when He seems absent.

- A crucial point in St. Teresa of Avila's example of prayer as drawing water from the well is that the water is for the plants. The water is our experience of God in prayer, often called consolations, and the plants in the garden are the virtues.

- Prayer, even for St. Teresa who was a contemplative, is not an end in itself. It is for the plants, the virtues.

b. We do not seek the experience of God in prayer merely for its own sake, but in order that the virtues in our lives may live and grow.
- We do not draw water from the well for the sheer joy of drawing it but in order to keep the plants alive and growing.
- St. Teresa's response to the question, "What should we do if our prayer is dry?" would be: "First pray, 'Lord, if this dryness is from something in me that needs to change, show me and I will try to change it. But unless and until You do, I will not entertain vague doubts.'" That is, I will not keep probing at myself for the cause.
- She would say, "Look at the flowers, the virtues, and see how they are doing. If the dryness is from God He keeps the flowers alive without the water!"

3. Some are called to witness to the Lord in redemptive suffering.
"So I persevere for the sake of those who are chosen, so that they, too, may obtain the salvation that is in Christ Jesus" (2 Tim 2:10).

a. By His death and resurrection, Jesus won victory over sin, Satan and death. The final outcome of victory is assured for those who believe in His name. However, He made the cross a condition for following Him.

"'If anyone wants to be a follower of mine, let him renounce himself and take up his cross and follow me'" (Mt 16:24).
- The question is not why Christ's followers suffer. The question is why we so often do not experience that the Lord is "with us" in our suffering.
- Paul says, "The temporary, light burden of our hardships is earning us for ever an utterly incomparable, eternal weight of glory" (2 Cor 4:17).

b. Jesus did not promise there would be no darkness. He promised to be a light in the valley of darkness. He promised to be with us.
- "God works with those who love him…and turns everything to their good" (Rom 8:28).
- In Acts 9, Paul is blinded until he can receive new insight into who God is. He got "sick" in Galatia, so he could stay to preach there (see Gal 4: 13-15), and he was shipwrecked off Malta so he would go there (see Acts 28:1-10).

4. Purification with Jesus in His Passion

"Let us keep our eyes fixed on Jesus…for the sake of the joy which lay ahead of him, he endured the cross, disregarding the shame of it" (Heb 12:2).

Each one of us has a place in the passion where our suffering corresponds with the suffering of Jesus.
- For some, it might be the moment in the Agony in the Garden, the experience of loneliness and betrayal by friends (see Lk 22:39-46).
- For others, Jesus before Pilate, the pain of false accusation and injustice (see Lk 23:1ff).
- For many, the fast of Jesus during His passion, the struggle with self-control especially under pressure (see Mt 27:34).
- For so many more, the physical pains of Jesus:
  - Those with headaches, sharing His crowning with thorns (see Mt 27: 27-29);
  - Those with backaches and joint pain, uniting with His carrying the cross, His falls (see Jn 19:17).
- For still others, Mary's passion, the death of a child, or a loved one (see Jn 19:25). Doing this we can share intimately in the passion of Jesus and find strength and peace in our own suffering.

Sheep may wander when the sun is shining, but when the sky grows dark and they hear the growling of wild animals they huddle close to their shepherds.

Unit II

More Power

Fan into flame…the Spirit
of power (2 Tim 1:6-7).

Session 4
More Power Through The Charisms

"You will receive the power of the Holy Spirit" (Acts 1:8).

Goals
1. To appreciate the value and variety of the charisms of the Holy Spirit.
2. To experience a further release of the charisms.

Framing Image
Many years ago a very poor family boarded a ship for the "New World." They brought cheese sandwiches and water for the voyage. Throughout the journey they stayed in the lower part of the ship eating their cheese sandwiches and water. Then one of the restless youngsters exploring the ship discovered there was a great banquet hall. As he peeked in, someone called to him, "Come in and eat. It goes with the passage!" After he enjoyed a great feast he returned to his family and urged them to come to the banquet. When some hesitated insisting, "We can't afford it," he exclaimed with delight, "It's free, it's absolutely free!" Some went and enjoyed all the rich foods, but others held back declaring they were satisfied with cheese sandwiches and water!

Key Point
The Father offers us a great banquet of gifts of the Spirit which was bought and paid for by the death of His Son. They are absolutely free! We don't earn them or deserve them. We simply need to be expectant and hungry, seeking and open to all that He has for us.

A. Love: Releases the charisms
1. Love motivates the charisms.
"Make love your aim; but be eager, too, for spiritual gifts" (1 Cor 14:1). That line, situated in the midst of Paul's teaching on the charisms, does not make the gifts a second rate alternative to love, but suggests that love has to be the motive for "Set your mind on the higher gifts" (1 Cor 12:31). To seek love is to highlight what ignites desire for the gifts.

2. Lack of desire stifles the charisms.

"Charisms are to be accepted with gratitude by the person who receives them and by all members of the Church as well" (*CCC*, 800).

a. The more we love Jesus the more we desire to let Him use us to bring others to know Him.

- The more we desire to be used, the more we recognize our need to be empowered with His gifts for ministry.

b. The more we love our family and recognize their need to know Jesus, the more we desire to be equipped with gifts of the Spirit to do this.

- Unless we know our need we will not desire, unless we desire we will not ask and unless we ask we will not receive!

c. The charisms do not come automatically. Four times in chapters 12–14 of 1 Corinthians, Paul uses a Greek word, *zealote*, which suggests a passionate desire and an active seeking of gifts.

- It implies that the charisms must be yearned for and prayed for.

3. Charisms express love.

"There was a dead man being carried out, the only son of his mother, and she was a widow.... When the Lord saw her he felt sorry for her and said...'Young man, I tell you: get up'" (Lk 7:12-14).

The charisms are the means the Spirit gives us to express the love of Christ in concrete and practical ways.

"They [charisms] are a wonderfully rich grace for the apostolic vitality and for the holiness of the entire Body of Christ, provided they really are...in keeping with charity, the true measure of all charisms" (*CCC*, 800).

a. The gift of tongues is a gift that expresses love because it is a gift for prayer. It lifts our hearts to God in a language purely for His praise, a language in which we have never offended Him.

- It is a gift that unites us so that we can pray in one voice in the Spirit (see Acts 2:4).

b. The gift of prophecy is a gift first for hearing and then for speaking the Word of God (1 Cor 14:3).

- The Spirit often speaks a word outside of ourselves through the gift of prophecy to break down our resistance to a word He has been trying to get through to us in our personal prayer.

c. The gift of healing reconciles and heals the wounds of unlove in our lives (see Mk 5:25-34).

4. Love purifies the charisms.
a. The charisms are stifled by not fostering their working together.
"Nor can the head say to the feet, 'I have no need of you'" (1 Cor 12:21).
- The gifts work together. Whenever Paul teaches on the gifts of the Spirit, he uses the analogy of the body. Without unselfishness, the gifts get sidetracked by self-interest, self-glorification and lose their power to build up the body of Christ.
- The gifts are left unused if some glance longingly and with dissatisfaction, coveting the gifts of others while not recognizing their own.
- On the other hand, the gifts can also be abused if people are arrogant about their gifts, not recognizing their need for the gifts of others.

b. Greater unity releases the power of the Spirit.
- If the branches are not in unity with one another, they cannot bear fruit. The same is true for the gifts of the Spirit. Unreconciled relationships stifle the free exercise of the gifts.
- On the other hand, deeper, more committed relationships give people a sense of belonging and the courage to take the risk of using a gift knowing they will be discerned and pruned by a loving community.

5. Love authenticates the charisms.
- In Matthew 7, Jesus speaks about love, about avoiding judgment, about treating others, as we would have them treat us.
- Then, to all who exercise spiritual gifts without love, Jesus says, "'When the day comes many will say to me, "Lord, Lord, did we not prophesy in your name, drive out demons in your name, work many miracles in your name?" Then I shall tell them to their faces: I have never known you; away from me, all evil doers!'" (Mt 7:22-23).
- Paul challenges the Corinthians' claim to be "spiritual" because they have these gifts. The truly spiritual person is the person of love. As long as there is jealousy and strife among them he tells them they are "a gong booming or a cymbal clashing" (1 Cor 13:1).

B. Power: Charisms and service
1. The charisms: power for mission
"'You will receive the power of the Holy Spirit which will come on you, and then you will be my witnesses ... to earth's remotest end'" (Acts 1:8).

The Greek word for power is *dunamis* from which we derive the word dynamite. The Holy Spirit is meant to be explosive in our lives.

a. **Being baptized in the Holy Spirit is meant to be more than a conversion experience.** It is meant to be an empowering call to go out and witness to Christ.
- In *Tertio Millennio Adveniente* (45) Pope John Paul II says, "In our own day too, the Spirit is the principal agent of the new evangelization."
- The charisms are an integral part of the mission of evangelization. Paul uses three words for the charisms; gifts, services and workings of power. They stress that the gifts are for the work of building up the Church.
- Without the charisms there is no power in evangelization.

b. **Failure to say "yes" to our mission stifles the charisms.**
- The gift of tongues is a gift for evangelization. When we do not know how to pray for someone the Spirit prays within us (see Rom 8:26).
- The gifts of prophecy, teaching, wisdom, understanding, and counsel are gifts for evangelization because the Spirit enables us to speak words that go beyond our human wisdom (see 1 Cor 14:24).
- The healing gifts are gifts for evangelization because the Lord uses signs and wonders to get the people's attention so He can speak to their hearts (see Acts 3).

2. **The variety of charisms for everyone**

a. **The charisms are stifled by too narrow a view of their variety and the various ways the Lord wants to use us with His gifts.**

We also need to pray for a fresh outpouring of the gifts of teaching, preaching, the gifts of faith, giving, mercy, of being helpers and administrators, the gifts of intercession and hospitality, the gifts of words of wisdom and knowledge, and the gifts of marriage, celibacy, voluntary poverty and even martyrdom.
- Don't limit God's activity to what seems like the supernatural activities. Charisms are concrete manifestations of the action of the Holy Spirit that are oriented towards service and the building up of the community. The gifts of administration, helping and giving are all charismatic gifts mentioned by St. Paul (see Rom 12:6-8).
- We need to recognize our natural gifts and abilities and ask God to empower them for greater service to the Body. A charism does not always have to be emotionally charged, it just has to be moved by the Spirit.
- The most important charisms that have been renewed are the fundamental charisms of our vocations in life. We need to recognize them as charisms, as empowerments by the Spirit and appropriate them anew.

b. **Limiting them to special people stifles charisms.**

"The particular manifestation of the Spirit granted to each one is to be used for the general good" (1 Cor 12:7).

- The charisms are not intended to be for a few people, but for everyone in the Body of Christ. The question is not, "Does the Lord want to give me gifts?" The questions are, "What gifts does He want to give me? How does He want me to exercise the charisms He gives me?"
- The charisms are gifts from God, the fruit of the death and resurrection of Jesus Christ. "God chose those who by human standards are…weak to shame the strong" (1 Cor 1:27). We need to let this recognition overcome a false humility that says we are too sinful, too unworthy or too ignorant to be used by God. They are gifts of the God who says, "'What father among you, if his son asked for a fish, would hand him a snake'" (Lk 11:11).

c. Limiting the variety of ways and places the Lord wants to use them stifles charisms.

Charisms are not just for charismatic prayer meetings. They are for life. Be open to surprises! Don't limit God's activity to our past experiences.

- A "word of knowledge" is an insight into a reality for practical decisions, not just for healing services. It is a gift for responding to problems with children, for counseling, for the Sacrament of Reconciliation.
- The gift of prophecy needs to be used in priests' assemblies, congregational meetings and parish meetings. The Lord wants us to be prophetic when it means speaking for unpopular Gospel principles. If there is a lack of prophets there is going to be a lack of conversion.
- We need to stir up the gift of teaching for homes, schools, and ministries in our parishes as well as our charismatic gatherings. If there is a lack of teachers there is going to be a lack of growth.
- Expect healing to happen in our homes when we pray with our children, in the Sacraments, in the healing ministries of our prayer groups, in our sharing groups, in our doctors' offices as we experience that extension of the Lord's healing ministry, and even on the telephone.

C. Wisdom: Charisms and maturity

We need wisdom and the discipline of self-control if we are to grow in the charisms.

1. Limiting them to when we were younger in the Spirit stifles the charisms.
Some say, "We don't need these spiritual gifts anymore. They were just for the beginning days of the Charismatic Renewal to get us started, but now that we have matured we don't need them anymore."

a. Charisms are for our ongoing growth and they should not diminish but, in fact, grow stronger as we mature.

- There is a change in the way we experience and use them as we mature. Often, the manifestations the Lord used in the beginning to get our attention stop.
- Each use of a spiritual gift becomes an act of faith, a kind of walking on water. This stepping out in faith is easy when we are still close to our initial experience of the Holy Spirit. Then God purifies us of our attachment to "good feelings" lest we value the gifts more than the Giver.

2. Our failure to give and accept correction in the use of them stifles the charisms.

"'Every branch that does bear fruit he prunes to make it bear even more'" (Jn 15:2).

a. The charisms need to be pruned so that they can flourish without being discredited by misuse.
- We ought to have both the willingness to give and the humility to accept correction.
- If the charisms are disciplined according to God's own mind, and used for the one purpose of revealing and glorifying Him, we will experience them as vital keys to the building of the Kingdom and they will remain as a permanent asset of the Church.

b. Our job is to learn how to use the charisms with a discipline that can release their fullest power, and at the same time, fulfill their true purpose.
- We are taught to seek the prophetic gifts, but we are also shown that prophecy is a heavy responsibility and that the prophets themselves should be the first to desire authoritative discernment (see 1 Cor 14:29-33).
- The charismatic gift of discernment, the gift to distinguish whether an "inspiration" is really from the Holy Spirit, needs to be stirred up.
- Likewise, the gift of pastoring, which is the gift to both encourage and prune the gifts, needs to be further developed.

3. Study the history of the charisms.

a. Being ashamed of them or too defensive about them stifles the charisms.
- Our need for acceptance can lead us to be ashamed of the charisms and to curtail them lest they keep people away.
- If one studies about the spiritual gifts throughout history one will know that the spiritual gifts are really in the teaching and history of the Church.
- It is important to know the statements of the Pope and Bishops on the spiritual gifts so that we are convinced of the support we have from the Church.

Session 5:
More Power Through Community

"Holy Father…so that they may be one like us" (Jn 17:11).

Goals
1. To become convinced that community is a necessary part of life in the Spirit.
2. To grow in knowing how to build committed relationships and heal broken relationships.

Framing Story
A pastor noticed that one of his parishioners had not come to church in a long time. When he visited the man they sat relaxing next to the charcoal fireplace. As they began the conversation the pastor removed one of the hot coals from the fire and set it off by itself. As they continued to chat about many things the coal slowly began to die out. When it had lost the last spark of its fire, the pastor excused himself and left. The man returned to church the following Sunday.

Key Point
Community is a necessary part of keeping the fire of the Holy Spirit alive in our lives. Each of us is like the coal that will lose its fire unless it remains with the others. Together we are like the coals that need to be piled one on top of the other if they are to produce a fire that will last.

A. Accept the call to community
1. We are community by our Baptism
In *Christifideles Laici* (10) Pope John Paul II says, "Baptism regenerates us in the life of the Son of God; unites us to Christ and to his Body, the Church." He then quotes St. Paul to say that "the result [of our being baptized into Christ] is that 'we, though many, are one body in Christ' (Rom 12:5)" (12).
- Growth in the Spirit means accepting that we are community first by God's action in us. Our responsibility is to become more fully what we already are.

2. The prayer of Jesus calls for community.
"'May they all be one, just as, Father, you are in me and I am in you, so that they also may be in us, so that the world may believe it was you who sent me'" (Jn 17:21).

The complete other-centeredness of the Trinity is our model of good relating. The Father shows the Son all that He does (see Jn 5:20). The Son always does what pleases the Father (see Jn 8:28–29). The Spirit takes the things of the Son and shows them to believers (see Jn 16:13-14).

3. The word and example of Jesus calls for community.
a. Loving one another is an integral part of the call to holiness.
"'This is my commandment: love one another, as I have loved you'" (Jn 15:12).
- We need to follow the example of Jesus. His bond with His disciples was a personal one, not a professional one. He valued them as persons, praying with them, sharing life and faith with them, sharing parties with them.
- They grew in unity with Him, but also with one another.

b. The Spirit of Jesus we have received is a communal Spirit drawing us into unity.
"The whole group of believers was united, heart and soul" (Acts 4:32).
- One of the greatest miracles of Pentecost was that the Apostles who were arguing before Pentecost (see Lk 22:24-27) were bonded together after they received the promised gift of the Spirit for unity.

c. Community is part of the way God calls us to witness to Him in the world.
"'It is by your love for one another, that everyone will recognize you as my disciples'" (Jn 13:35).
- The disciples after Pentecost witnessed first by the unity of their lives.

4. The Church calls for community.
In *Christifideles Laici* Pope John Paul II insists, "Small basic...communities are true expressions of ecclesial communion and centers of evangelization" (26) and as such are a vital part of the renewal of Christian life.
- Community is an integral part of the way God intends us to grow. The Latin root of the word community is *munio* which means to "to fortify."

5. Our human need calls for community.
The growing number of support groups for all varieties of needs shows the increasing recognition in society that the human touch is needed in the midst of the increasing de-personalization of society.

6. The experience in the Charismatic Renewal points to the need for community.
"Baptism in the Holy Spirit introduces those who have known it to an experience of Christian community that transcends anything they have previously known" (*Fanning the Flame*, p. 13).

Community has always been recognized as important in the Charismatic Renewal. From the days of the first "Life in The Spirit Seminar," community has been one of the "spokes" on the wheel of growth.
- For a while a prayer meeting offers a smaller, more personal opportunity for relationships than most parishes offer.
- Then needs change. People begin looking for more. There is often an "is-this-all-there-is?" feeling, an incompleteness that sends people looking for community elsewhere.
- People often don't stay with the prayer group after the "Life in the Spirit Seminar" because they miss the small discussion groups.
- Human tensions lead to disunity because there is no place to resolve conflict.
- People share too long and too soon in the prayer meeting because they are looking for a place to share their burdens.

B. Build committed relationships.
1. The model of loving
Beginning with the model that the Trinity gives, a good relationship in community (including marriage) is one in which the members willingly and actively devote themselves to the well being of each other.

a. Self-centeredness is then our basic sin against one another in community.
It cannot be easily defined nor is it the same for everyone.
- Blending the different personalities in a community can be like conducting an orchestra. The trumpets with their bold strong sounds and the violins with their gentle soft tones are both important to a musical composition. However, too much of one and not enough of the other can ruin the harmony.

b. Self-centeredness can be self-centered assertiveness.
- For the "trumpets" in the community the call to become more other-centered is a call to hold back and to care for others by learning to listen more.

c. Self-centeredness can be self-centered conformity.
- For the "violins" becoming more other-centered means learning to come out more, to share more.

A line from Paul's letter to the Thessalonians gives a framework for developing these different aspects of the call to love one another in community.

> "**Admonish those who are undisciplined, encourage the apprehensive, support the weak and be patient with everyone**" (1 Thes 5:14).

2. Love is caring.

"Support the weak" is also translated "help" or "care for." Caring cannot be guessed at. It needs to be shown in signs that the other will recognize.

a. Listening

Real caring begins when someone loves enough to want to hear and takes time to listen with the heart.

- So many people spend time pretending to manage and keep up a smile because no one seems ready to listen. Others do irritating things to get our attention because they are crying out for someone to care enough to listen.
- Caring calls for listening to the feelings of others beneath the surface of their words and actions. It is not too difficult to listen to another's words but to hear all of him or her we have to listen to their feelings and this is not easy. It calls for listening with feeling, concern and love.
- We can be too busy doing things for people to really hear them. We can fix people's ideas and problems before we know them. We can finish their sentences, "I know just what you mean" and tell our story or give answers when what they need is simply our presence.
- While Peter was still denying Him, Jesus looked straight at him with love. Jesus listened beneath the surface of Peter's words to what He knew was in Peter's heart (see Lk 22:61).

b. Compassion

The fruit of listening is compassion. Compassion is to "suffer with" the other, to find some point of connection with another, to recognize something of ourselves in that person enabling us to say, "I know your pain, and I know your joy."

St. Peter exhorts: "Since…you can experience the genuine love of brothers, love each other intensely from the heart" (1 Pt 1:22).

- To be compassionate is to enter into our own hearts and, while knowing ourselves to be different than God expects or desires us to be, to know that we are loved and lovable.
- It is to find there the motivation and the freedom to reach out to every other person, also different than God desires them to be yet loved and lovable.
- The compassionate heart does not condemn but recognizes how each person's story connects with his or her own.

"Do not judge, and you will not be judged…. Why do you observe the splinter in your brother's eye and never notice the great log in your own?" (Mt 7:1-3).

c. Encouragement

"Encourage the apprehensive." Compassion leads to appreciation and appreciation overflows into encouragement.

- To encourage is to give heart to, to affirm the gifts and abilities of one another. When we listen we discover each person is carrying a gift that he or she wants to reveal to anyone who shows genuine interest.
- We need to affirm not just with words but also with our emotional warmth. So much can be said, so much healed with a hug.
- Many sources of disunity in our relationships are coming from basic needs for encouragement and appreciation. The Lord wants us to be ministers of such encouragement and appreciation to one another.

3. Love is sharing.
"For this is how God loved the world: he gave his only Son, so that everyone who believes in him may not perish but may have eternal life" (Jn 3:16).

The Father shared what was most dear to Him, His well-beloved Son. Jesus did the same. Jesus shared with the apostles His moments of glory on Tabor as well as His moments of sorrow at Gethsemane. He shared all of Himself with us.

a. Put a priority on sharing our lives.
- Our life with God is the most important thing we have in common. We need to talk about our prayer life, our experiences with God.

b. Be vulnerable with one another.
- Share our struggles and our successes, our hopes and moments of near despair, our acts of courage and our real fears, our joys and sorrows especially as these are being used by God as signs of His grace in our lives.
- Weakness that is shared is a blessing drawing us closer together; weakness that refuses to be dealt with is an obstacle to unity. If we would only acknowledge our woundedness to one another so much that separates us would be healed.

If we have the heart to listen and to share with the compassion and patience of Jesus, we will be healing communities to one another and the need to repair relationships will be greatly decreased. However, even with the best and sincerest efforts to build community of heart, problems among people will arise.

C. Heal broken relationships.
1. Love is bearing.
"Carry each other's burdens; that is how to keep the law of Christ" (Gal 6:2). We bear one another's burdens by continual forgiveness.

a. Forgiveness sets us free, "Like a bird from the fowlers' net" (Ps 124:7). (This is also translated "hunters' cage.")
- In forgiving we appropriate the freedom Jesus has won for us. By His

saving grace Jesus took the door off the cage so we don't have to be in bondage in any way.
- Bearing grudges keeps us bound and out of the Father's house like the unforgiving elder brother of the prodigal son (See Lk 15:25-32).

b. Forgiveness is a decision, not a feeling.
- If we decide to forgive the Holy Spirit will empower us to forgive. If we desire to forgive the Holy Spirit will give us the strength to decide to forgive.
- We need to use the cross of Jesus as our inspiration and pray, "Lord, how can I refuse to forgive when you didn't refuse to forgive on the cross?" The cross of Jesus is our sins; our cross is often one another's sins.

c. We need to forgive as the Lord has forgiven us.
"Bear with one another; forgive each other if one of you has a complaint against another. The Lord has forgiven you; now you must do the same" (Col 3:13).
- The Lord's forgiveness is unconditional. It is forgiving without waiting to be asked, without waiting for justification, without waiting even for an acknowledgement of the hurt.
- To forgive as the Lord has forgiven us is also to forgive and forget. To forget does not mean suppressing the memory; it means not rerunning, rehearsing and nursing the hurt. It means to "bring every thought into captivity and obedience to Christ" (2 Cor 10:5).

2. Love is confronting.
"Admonish those who are undisciplined."

A key element in preserving unity is being able to recognize problems that arise from different personalities and expectations, from individual past hurts and from fears and aggressions.

"So from now on, there must be no more lies. Speak the truth to one another, since we are all parts of one another" (Eph 4:25).

a. The most loving thing to do is to deal with problems directly.
- If we mask tensions and try to pretend they do not exist, they come out indirectly in irritated tones, abruptness or avoidance. If we deal with them indirectly, such as teaching on a problem, frequently the wrong people take the word seriously and those who most need to hear it miss the point.

b. Dealing with tensions directly does not mean hasty confrontation.
- Making a tension explode does not resolve it. They need to be handled with sensitivity and a great deal of patience.

"Take every care to preserve the unity of the Spirit by the peace that binds you together" (Eph 4:3).

c. Tensions bring us back to the reality of our helplessness.
- Tensions oblige us to spend more time in prayer ministry and dialogue to overcome the crisis. We are reminded that our community is more than a human reality, that it needs the Spirit of God to deepen it.

If our goal is love, we embrace in order to heal; if our goal is perfection, we exclude in order to perfect.

3. Love is patient.
"Be patient with everyone." Patience is manifesting forbearance under provocation.

a. Patience with one another is purification.
- We can be ready for purification from without because it can make us feel like heroes, martyrs. But when purification comes from within our family, our prayer group or our community, we often complain and resist it.

b. Patience is rooted in reverence.
- "Regard others as more important than yourself" (Rom 12:10). The Greek word for "regard" is sometimes translated "honor" or "esteem" or "respect" or "reverence." Reverence is ordinarily a word ascribed to God alone. To speak of reverence for one another is to recognize that each person is only a little less than the angels (see Ps 8) (NAB), a reflection of God wondrously made by Him in his or her mother's womb (see Ps 139).

Session 6
More Power Through Service

"I commissioned you to go out and to bear fruit,
fruit that will last" (Jn 15:16).

Goals
1. To stir up zeal and boldness for service.
2. To develop some skills for evangelization.

Framing Story
Years ago there was a wealthy man who, with his devoted son, shared a passion for art collecting. Together they traveled the world adding the finest art treasures to their collection. As winter approached, war engulfed the nation and the young man left to serve his country. A few weeks later his father received news that his beloved son died while saving a fellow soldier's life. The old man faced the upcoming Christmas holidays with anguish and sadness.

On Christmas morning, the depressed father was awakened by a young soldier who greeted him saying, "I'm the one your son was rescuing when he died. I'm not a great artist but I want to give you this picture of your son which I drew." That painting became the one the father valued most and which he placed in the center of his great art treasures.

The following spring the old man died and left in his will that his paintings were to be auctioned off on Christmas morning, the day he had received his greatest gift.

The auction began with the painting of the man's son. The art dealers objected and none would bid on what they considered a piece of junk. Finally a man serving there, who was too poor to bid anything, asked if he could have it, for he knew and loved the man and his son. The auctioneer rapped the gavel. "Gone," he said and then "The auction is over!" Over the objections of the great art collectors, the auctioneer said, "According to the will of the father, whoever takes the picture of his son gets all the great art treasures as well!"

Key Point
The Father not only calls us to serve as His Son did, but He also equips us with all His gifts to continue the mission He sends us on. Our response is not an option. The fruit of the vine (see Jn 15) is not for the branches, it is for the hungry. It will wither and die if it is not plucked and eaten. The same is true

with the gifts and fruits of the Spirit. Unless we let the Lord use us, the life of the Spirit in us will die.

A. Called to zeal
1. The zeal of Jesus
Jesus was consumed with zeal for His Father's work. "'Did you not know that I must be in my Father's house'" (Lk 2:49). "I am eaten up with zeal for your house" (Jn 2:17).

2. The zeal of the early Church.
The one hundred and twenty disciples gathered at Pentecost received the same Holy Spirit we have received and they evangelized the whole known world. Why was it so important to the early Church to evangelize?

a. Because of God's love—They took seriously the words of Jesus, "'Do you love me?'... 'Feed my sheep'" (Jn 21:15-17). They were so in love with Jesus they were ready to give everything to make Him known.
- We need to fall so in love with Jesus so that we can say with St. Paul, "Preaching the gospel gives me nothing to boast of, for I am under compulsion and I should be in trouble if I failed to do it" (1 Cor 9:16).

b. Because of Christ's command—They took seriously the farewell words of Jesus, "'Go...make disciples of all nations'" (Mt 28:19).
- We need to take this as a command not as a suggestion and let the Holy Spirit use us. Have we used God and not let Him use us?

c. Because it brought them such joy—Paul could say to the Thessalonians, "What do you think is our hope and our joy, and what our crown of honour in the presence of our Lord Jesus when he comes? You are, for you are our pride and joy" (1 Thes 2:19-20).
- The greatest joy for a Christian is bringing someone else to know Jesus who didn't know Jesus before. If we don't have the joy of the Lord or don't have the joy we had in the beginning, is it because we are not witnessing to Jesus?

d. Because of their trust in the Holy Spirit—When Paul was invited by King Agrippa to make his defense, his response showed he knew the source of all the power of his ministry: "It is for my hope in the promise made by God to our ancestors that I am on trial" (Acts 26:6).
- Trust releases the power of God to act in us.

e. Because of their sense of responsibility—"We are ambassadors for Christ" (2 Cor 5:20).

- They considered serving a privilege and felt accountable for the gifts (see Eph 3:7ff).

B. Gifted with the Spirit
1. Jesus depended on the anointing of the Holy Spirit.
In the Gospel of Luke, Jesus gives us His mission statement: "'The spirit of the Lord is on me, for he has anointed me to bring the good news to the afflicted. He has sent me to proclaim liberty to captives, sight to the blind, to let the oppressed go free, to proclaim a year of favour from the Lord'" (Lk 4:18-19).

2. Let the Spirit empower us for service.
The Spirit was not given to make us comfortable. It was given to make us missionaries, to equip us to serve the Church in its primary mission of evangelization.

"You will receive the power of the Holy Spirit…and then you will be my witnesses" (Acts 1:8).

3. Let love overcome fear.
a. Fear of our inadequacy — When Paul came to the Corinthians he came among them "in weakness, in fear and great trembling and what I spoke and proclaimed was not meant to convince by philosophical argument, but to demonstrate the convincing power of the Spirit, so that your faith should depend not on human wisdom but on the power of God" (1 Cor 2:3-5).
- Paul had just left Athens where he had failed to make converts because he had depended on his human abilities.
- God wants our availability not our capability.

b. Fear of failure — Jesus wants to free us of our fear of failure.
- He guarantees we will fail and assures us that we are in good company because some of His extended family, the rich young man and even some of His disciples turned away. "'No prophet is ever accepted in his own country'" (Lk 4:24).

c. Fear of seeming superior — can appear to be humility; but it is false humility.
- We can be afraid of giving the appearance of being better than others.
- If we witness out of a realization that evangelization is one beggar showing another beggar where the bread is, we will not appear superior.

d. Fear of getting involved — We know witnessing is costly.
- It takes time, effort, consistent living. It will require prayer, caring, attention to the Word of God and spiritual warfare.

- We may feel cold and empty; but witnessing is not a reward for holiness. It is a means to it. The Lord ministers to us as we minister to others.

e. **Fear of rejection**—the word "witness" in Greek is the same as the word for martyr.
- Jesus made it clear that if we are going to follow Him, we can expect rejection. He was despised and rejected of men (see Is 53:1-3).
- "He came to his own and his own people did not accept him" (Jn 1:11).
- The servant is not different than the master.

C. Sent to be effectively evangelistic
"Proclaim the Lord Christ holy in your hearts, and always have your answer ready for people who ask you the reason for the hope that you have" (1 Pt 3:15).

St. Peter exhorts us to proclaim the Lord not only by the witness of our lives, but also by our witness in words. That is the call of our Holy Father at the beginning of this third millennium.

"To nourish ourselves with the word in order to be 'servants of the word' in the work of evangelization: this is surely a priority for the Church at the dawn of the new millennium" (*Novo Millennio Ineunte,* 40).

To respond we need to overcome a false idea of evangelization. It is not standing on a street corner on a box or in a huge stadium talking to the multitudes. That is the ministry of the evangelist. It is not everyone's call, but to evangelize is.

1. Three ways to evangelize:
a. Start a conversation.
Philip in his conversation with the Ethiopian is an example of how to let a conversation become a witness (see Acts 8:26-40).
- He listened first. He asked the eunuch, who was reading the book of Isaiah, if he understood what he was reading. Witnessing starts first by listening, not by speaking.
- Philip met him where he was and led him to the point where he was asking for instruction. Philip explained that the suffering servant was Jesus and led him to baptism.

Do we listen to another person, share their sorrows and let the conversation become an opportunity to witness? Or, do we add our troubles to theirs?

b. Give a witness.
A witness has three parts:
- what my life was like before God touched me;

- what Jesus in the power of the Holy Spirit did for me;
- what difference did He make. What my life is like now.
- Speak from personal experience. The blind man is a good example of this. The Pharisees questioned him about the authority of Jesus. He knew enough not to get into a theological discussion with them that was beyond his understanding. He said simply, "'All I know is that I was blind and now I can see'" (Jn 9:25).
- We can become discouraged if we attempt to respond to theological questions that are beyond us.
- Witness to Jesus and the power of the Spirit not to the Charismatic Renewal or the prayer group. They are only vehicles the Lord uses.
- Be real, not super-spiritual. Constantly speaking "God-talk" turns people off. Use normal language, not lingo such as "born again," "saved," "tongues," "slain in the spirit."
- Be gentle, be patient.

c. Extend an invitation

Some of the best disciples were won to Jesus by a simple invitation, "Come and see." It is the easiest form of evangelization.

For "extend an invitation" evangelization to be effective, however, we need to ensure that our gatherings are places where Jesus is alive and being proclaimed.

2. Participate in prayer meetings that evangelize.

A charismatic prayer meeting evangelizes if it is vibrant! It will be vibrant if each person goes ready to be used by the Spirit, thinking "Yes, use me, Lord."

a. Be a participant, not an observer.

Sitting on the perimeter of the prayer circle or in the back indicates an attitude of being an observer. Move to the center or the front and be a participant.

b. Enter into praise and worship.

- Speak out in praise! Each person's voice is an instrument played in a symphony of praise.
- Sing with the music. "Those who sing pray twice" (St. Augustine). Pray and sing in the Spirit with the charismatic gift of tongues.
- "Shout for joy" (Ps 32:11). We shout at ball games, then why are we timid in raising our voices for Jesus? Overcome the fear of looking foolish, of releasing feelings.
- Let your body praise the Lord. Raising our hands is a form of proclaiming Jesus as our Lord. "Stretch out your hands…and bless Yahweh" (Ps 134:2). Be faithful to persevering praise based on commitment, not feeling.

c. **Proclaim the Word of God. It has the power to evangelize.**
- Scripture—Be prepared with your scripture to read a word that fits in with the theme the Lord is developing in the prayer meeting.
- Prophecy, Word of Knowledge—Wait expectantly after the word of praise. It is the pregnant pause when the Lord often speaks a word. Be ready to be used for prophecy and then submit to the discernment of the community.
- Teaching, witnessing—Give short ten to fifteen minute witnesses and teachings to continue the evangelizing effort and growth of the prayer meeting.
- People go where they are fed.

d. **Intercede in an evangelistic way.**
If we pray not only for our own needs, but also all those who share the same sorrows and burdens, even our intercession can be evangelistic.

3. Evangelistic opportunities before and after the prayer meeting

a. **Meeting and greeting**—Hospitality is one of the greatest evangelistic opportunities of the prayer meeting.
- Evangelize by welcoming and putting a person at ease, explaining what to expect in the prayer meeting. Follow-up afterward to answer questions can make the difference in whether or not a person returns.

b. **Healing prayer**—People are most open to hear the Word of God when they are in need.
- Be open to praying for people and expect the Lord to use you in healing teams. Healing teams need people who pray, who are committed members of the group, who are able to keep confidentiality and who can surrender burdens of others back to the Lord.

c. **Faith sharing groups**—It is not enough to bring people to an isolated experience of meeting Jesus.
- We need to connect them to the community of Christians.

d. **Initiation teaching**—Life in the Spirit Seminars are an essential part of the ongoing evangelization of a prayer meeting.
- Become part of a Life in the Spirit Seminar team and let the new life in the Spirit grow as the Lord uses you to bring others into that life.
- Get the word out about the seminar. Ask the pastor to put a notice in the parish bulletin. Put flyers on the bulletin boards in supermarkets, in the college dormitories. Put an ad in the local newspaper. Be creative in getting out the good news that Jesus is alive and coming to the seminar!

e. Evangelistic breakfasts, Sabbath suppers, picnics and informal gatherings are often the way to evangelize people who would not come to prayer meetings.
- We need to mix witnessing with opportunities for relaxation. Don't be too spiritual about what evangelizes!

f. Acting with justice—Have a missionary outreach in the corporal works of mercy.
- Feed the hungry, clothe the naked, visit the imprisoned, and care for the sick.

Unit Three

More Wisdom

Stir into flame the gift of God…The Spirit God has given us…makes us…wise (2 Tim 1:6-7) (NAB).

Session 7
More Wisdom Through Discernment

"The Holy Spirit, whom the Father will send in my name, will teach you everything" (Jn 14:26).

Goals
1. To grow in understanding of the general ways God leads us.
2. To learn to discern specific inspirations of the Spirit.

Framing Story
The Ant and the Contact Lens
A young woman accepted an invitation to go rock climbing with her friends. She took hold of the rope and started up the face of the rock. When she reached a ledge to rest, a safety rope snapped against her eye and knocked out her contact lens. In desperation she asked the Lord to help her find it. She looked and looked but it was nowhere to be found. When she got to the top she sat down and looked out across the mountains, thinking "Lord, you know every stone and leaf of these mountains, so you know exactly where my contact lens is. Help me find it!" As she started down the mountain again a new group of climbers reached the top. One of them shouted out, "Hey, anybody lose a contact lens, we found an ant carrying it?"

The young woman drew a cartoon to witness to the incredible story. She drew a picture of an ant lugging that contact lens with the words, "Lord, I don't know why You want me to carry this thing. I can't eat it, and it's awfully heavy. But if this is what you want me to do, I'll carry it for you."

Key Point
The ways the Lord leads us are at times very unclear. We need to intently seek to discover His will while doing things we don't understand, trusting He will make the way clear.

A. Listening: Attitudes we need to hear God's will.
1. Faith Conviction
a. We need faith that God wants us to know His will.
"'If you ask me for anything in my name, I will do it'" (Jn 14:14).

- Knowing God's will is not a hide and seek game. His will is as clear as the faith we have to believe it to be.

b. Faith that God is present revealing his will.
- Heartfelt conviction that He is alive and that He directs us not simply in general sets of principles for Christian life but in specific directions for our daily life.

2. Faith Knowledge

a. Growth in spiritual thinking. "Putting on the mind of Christ" is the best way of knowing His will (see Rom 12:2).
- God guides not only by inspiration, heart knowledge, but also by principle, head knowledge.

b. A life of discernment requires prayer and study.
- We need to spend time with Him, His Word, His Spirit.
  "Be rooted in him" (Col 2:7).
  The gifts of grace must form a unity with the gifts of intelligence.

3. Hunger to Conform to the Will of God

a. Submit our wills to His Will.
- We need to decide to obey God's will before He reveals it. If we are clinging to our own will we are not sensitive to the Spirit.
- Sometimes, like Mary in the garden (see Jn 20:11-18), we are weeping because we are clinging to our will and not seeking God's will.

b. Surrender our lives to Him.
- Jesus needs to be Lord of our lives without qualifications.
- We need to surrender our desires, so God can reveal His purposes without struggling against our stubborn human wills.
  "'This people's heart has grown coarse, their ears dulled, they have shut their eyes tight to avoid using their eyes to see, their ears to hear, their heart to understand, changing their ways and being healed by me'" (Mt 13:15-17).

4. Spirit of recollection

We need to learn an ongoing sensitivity to His presence.
- Be present enough to the Lord to stop and pray when obstacles come, to ask, "Lord, what are you saying in these circumstances?"
- In agitation we can't perceive the gentle action of the Spirit.

B. Knowing: Objective criteria for testing the Spirit
1. His Teachings
a. Word of God in Scripture
- The Word of God is absolutely true and no genuine inspiration of the Holy Spirit will ever contradict it
- The doctrines and laws that have been given to us in the Word of God form a kind of framework within which we are called to live the life of the Spirit.
- Laziness or "super-spiritualism" results in seeking guidance on something clearly directed by God's word.

b. Word of God in Christian tradition
- A Catholic, in weighing an inspiration, should ask if it is in accord with the teaching of the Church.
- Tradition, spiritual writings and the spoken word of the Body of Christ today that have been positively affirmed, adopted throughout the Church, and firmly held for a long period of time become the surest guide the individual can have to the right sense of Christ's teaching.
"'Anyone who listens to you listens to me; anyone who rejects you rejects me, and those who reject me reject the one who sent me'" (Lk 10:16). Jesus said this when sending the disciples forth to preach.
- The teachings of the Church today are the continuation of the teaching of the Apostles.

2. General life direction
The commitments and responsibilities we have because of our vocation give us helpful criteria by which to judge an inspiration.
- God does not contradict Himself and does not inspire conflicting obligations. He does not inspire a married person to neglect his or her family responsibilities to go to a foreign mission.

3. Specific leadings or inspirations
Inner urgings or inspirations are irresistible inclinations that persist or persistent ideas that we can't seem to ignore.
- The Lord often guides us through our own inclinations. His will is usually not "the hard will of God" we have often believed it to be. "Make Yahweh your only joy and he will give you your heart's desires" (Ps 37:4).

There are two types of inspiration, the ordinary and the charismatic.

a. Ordinary inspirations

The ordinary inspirations of the Holy Spirit do not involve anything miraculous. They are experienced simply as urgings to act or not to act.

- When the Holy Spirit would not allow St. Paul to preach in Asia (see Acts 16:6), this seems to have been by way of an ordinary inspiration, without any message. St. Paul perhaps sensed deep within himself that preaching there was not what God wanted of him. His own reason had sent him on this apostolic journey (see Acts 15:36), but his heart somehow knew in a way of its own that this was not what God wanted.
- An individual might have a sudden impulse to call a family member or acquaintance with a special sense of the Lord's loving care of that person.
- The loving power of the Spirit might envelop a person to give them assurance and strength for a difficult task that confronts them.

b. Charismatic inspirations

These have the character of messages coming to us from a source other than ourselves. They take on various forms:

- A vision—St. Peter's vision of the clean and unclean animals in Acts 10:11ff.
- A word spoken—the words, "Take and eat," heard by Peter on that same occasion. It makes no great difference whether the words are really heard by the ears or are only interiorly sensed.
- A strong impulse to do a certain definite thing that one would not normally be inclined to do. Thus a person may be impelled to speak to a certain stranger, or to go to a place he or she would have no natural reason to visit.

Charismatic inspirations seem to be necessary when very explicit directions need to be given, or when a person is called to do something quite out of the ordinary because the ordinary inspirations are too vague to be able to carry such a message.

- Paul wandered about through the country uncertain what to do next. When the moment was right, Paul saw a vision of a Macedonian saying, "'Come across to Macedonia and help us'" (Acts 16:9). With that he knew where God was calling him.
- Since Paul had no natural contact with the Macedonians, it apparently was not possible for him to be drawn to Macedonia by an ordinary inspiration; instead, he was given a charismatic vision with specific directions.

C. Hearing: Subjective criteria for testing inspirations

Discernment of spirits has to do with determining whether the inspirations or impulses that come into our minds originate from the Holy Spirit, the human spirit or the evil spirit. Christ promised, "'The Holy Spirit, whom the Father will send in my name, will teach you everything and remind you of all I have said to you'" (Jn 14:26).

The subjective criteria are the ways we discern these inspirations.

1. The Fruits of the Spirit (Gal 5)

We need to recognize peace, love, joy and humility or the lack of these as signs or pointers to being in God's will or not.

a. Peace—When we are moving in accord with the will of God, there is a deep spirit of peace that fills us.

- Peace comes from being in right order. Hence, when we are "in His Will," we will be at peace even though we are encountering resistance and conflict exteriorly, or experiencing turmoil and anguish interiorly.

b. Love—Whatever is from God is ultimately motivated by love.

- Someone might feel impelled to do something that involves a more or less hostile confrontation with others. For example, one might feel called to correct their mistakes, to argue against their ideas, or to oppose their proposals. When this occurs, he or she should pause to check whether this is being done in a spirit of love.

c. Joy—When we have finally made our decision, we may experience a delicate joy that reassures us that the decision was right.

- Joy is often the one sign by which true holiness can be discriminated from false. Authentic Christianity always has joy in it, even for those who suffer much.
- The joylessness that is a negative sign is not that of a person momentarily overcome by grief but that of the one who has become habitually reluctant to embrace joy.

These signs ought to occur together in any genuine work of God. They are an important check on one another. False joy can be detected because it is lacking in peace; false peace will be wanting in love and humility, and so on.

2. The Word of God

Scripture opened to spontaneously and the gift of prophecy can be used by God to direct us or confirm a direction given in another way.

- We need to avoid turning to a word in Scripture before every move and using Scripture and prophecy as a sole guide.

3. Circumstances
a. Even the world around us is used by God to teach and guide us.
He has a way of putting all sorts of blocks in our path when we are bent upon the wrong thing, and of smoothing out the way for us in the most astonishing and inexplicable manner when we hit upon the right path.

"We are well aware that God works with those who love him, those who have been called in accordance with his purpose, and turns everything to their good" (Rom 8:28).
- We can pray, "Lord, show us by circumstances opening up clearly."
- It is the wisdom of Gamaliel who advised the elders, "'What I suggest, therefore, is that you leave these men alone and let them go. If this enterprise, this movement of theirs [Christianity], is of human origin it will break up of its own accord; but if it does in fact come from God you will be unable to destroy them. Take care not to find yourselves fighting against God'" (Acts 5:38-39).

b. The danger in relying solely on this is being too passive.
- "If a job turns up I'll work, otherwise I'll keep praying for one." We need to find a balance between active seeking and patient waiting.
- The prayer of St. Ignatius is a good example of this balance, "Take Lord, and receive my memory, my understanding, my entire will. Everything is yours, do with it what you will. Give me only your love and your grace, that is enough for me."

4. Community discernment
If possible, submit to a body sensitive to His Spirit. God has not called us as isolated individuals, but as members of a people
- We should seek His light, not merely by scrutinizing our own consciences, but also by consulting others qualified to guide us and, in a special way, the community of which we are a part.

5. Testing a decision
We can stay with one decision for a while, asking what is the fruit of the decision. Does the inclination grow stronger? Does peace follow? Does it draw us closer to the Lord? Or, do we feel an uneasiness, indecision and still feel drawn

to another possibility? Do we have a vague sense of resisting the Lord with many excuses?

D. The Charismatic Gift of Discernment
The charismatic gift of discernment (see 1 Cor 12:10) is the gift given by the Holy Spirit to be used by an individual to distinguish what is of the Spirit or not of the Spirit for another person or group.

    a. This charism or gift of the Spirit helps a community differentiate between evil spirits and good spirits.

    b. The signs indicating the validity of such a gift are the same objective and subjective criteria used in discernment in an individual's life: a life-style centered in the Lord, allegiance to Scripture and Church teaching, and willingness to die to self in the service of others.

E. Waiting on the Lord
"'Write the vision down…although it may take some time, wait for it, for come it certainly will before too long'" (Hab 2:2-3).

The last basic attitude necessary for discernment is willingness to wait on the Lord. Impetuosity in following out our impulses is one of the biggest obstacles to being led by the Spirit and one of the surest signs of not being led by Him. God does not drive us like an irresistible force. He gently solicits and leads. So, we frequently need to wait and pray to be sure it is He who is calling us.

Session 8
More Wisdom Through Vision

Having begun in the Spirit, can you be so stupid as to end in the flesh? (Gal 3:3)

Goals
1. To have a clarity about the identity and mission of the Catholic Charismatic Renewal.
2. To understand some challenges facing the Catholic Charismatic Renewal in the Church and the world today.

Framing Story
A talented young man entered a monastery eager to use his gifts for the glory of God. The Abbot told him, "First, go dig in the field." A year later he returned to the Abbot hoping he could now use his talent to compose music and sing for the Lord. He was told, "Go dig in the field." After a second year he returned to the Abbot eager this time to be able to paint beautiful images of Jesus and Mary. Again he was told, "Go dig in the field." When he was digging in the field he found a box full of pictures of monks singing, painting, dancing and using all their gifts for the Lord. He returned to the Abbot to tell him he was leaving to look for the monastery in the pictures and join it. As the young man left, the Abbot looked at the pictures and recognized himself as a young man with the founding community of his monastery. He sadly realized that they had lost the original vision that had brought them together and attracted young men like the one that had just left.

Key Point
The empowering effect of the Catholic Charismatic Renewal in the Church and the world today can be lost if we don't keep a clear vision of its identity and a clear sense of its mission.

A. Developing a common vision
"Where there is no vision the people get out of hand" (Pro 29:18) or become demoralized.

1. The importance of a common vision
Without a common vision a movement, a community or a prayer group may

find themselves working at cross purposes and building up more and more tensions.
- A vital reason for Jesus' success was that He came with a divine purpose. He was the possessor and proclaimer of a clear spiritual vision.

2. The elements of a common vision
Vision is a call from the Lord for a particular way of life or ministry. It is a way to live the Gospel. It is a direction for a group to go in.

A common vision has two aspects: clarity of identity and clarity of mission.
a. Clarity of identity gives a group a sense of who they are and is a key element of unity and growth.
- Often problems arise that do not yield to efforts at reconciliation because the problem is not a relationship problem (unity of heart), but a vision problem (unity of mind).

b. Clarity of mission gives a group a sense of why they are and is a key element of commitment to service.
- The vision they share must be great enough and clear enough to call forth commitment. No one will give up other things unless he/she sees something worth sacrificing for.

B. The Vision of the Catholic Charismatic Renewal in the Church and the World
We can move from the Spirit into the flesh if we limit the Charismatic Renewal to particular forms, structures or manifestations of the Spirit.

1. What the Catholic Charismatic Renewal is not.
a. It is not a movement like other movements.
Cardinal Suenens, the great supporter of the Charismatic Renewal from its earliest days, said, "To interpret the Renewal as a 'movement' among other movements is to misunderstand its nature; it is a movement of the Spirit offered to the entire Church and destined to rejuvenate every face of the Church's life" ("Pentecostal Refreshment for All Christians," *Goodnews*, July/August 1996).
- **There are no founders** — We celebrate as the anniversary of the Catholic Charismatic Renewal an "event" in 1967 in Pittsburgh, USA, but this manifestation of the Spirit occurred separately in other places without a direct connection to the beginnings in the USA.
- **There is no rule of life, no constitution; it is not spirituality.**
  It is not like Dominican, Franciscan, Ignatian spirituality that is for some

people according to their leanings. It is a move of the Spirit that gives new life and understanding to the various forms of spirituality.
- **There is no precise structure.** There is an international council and office in Rome to provide services to the Catholic Charismatic Renewal. However they do not give ecclesial structure to the movement The statutes of International Catholic Charismatic Renewal Services (ICCRS) are for the council of ICCRS.
- **It is not a prayer movement or a form of prayer.** There is a common form of prayer but Charismatic Renewal is much more than a way praying. It is a way of life. It is not essential to join a prayer group to be baptized in the Spirit.
- **There are no particular outward manifestations that are essential.** We raise our hands in prayer not because we have decided to adopt that form of prayer but because we desire to pray with our whole body.
- **Being emotional is not essential.** If emotion enters into the praise it is not because the individual is by nature emotional but rather as a response to God's love, as an overflow in verbal praise of God's greatness.

b. The purpose of the Catholic Charismatic Renewal is not to bring the Church into the "movement."
It is meant to be a vehicle of bringing new life in the Spirit into the Church. Again, Cardinal Suenens used to say it was like a "quickening river" coming down from the mountains and flowing into the sea. He urged that our "constant preoccupation should be that the waters of the river flow into the sea in loyalty to their source" (article as above).
- People who become discouraged by numbers dropping in prayer groups and conferences often miss this understanding. Rather than seeing their prayer group members as bringing new life to numerous ministries in the Church they feel abandoned.
- Our greater concern needs to be making our prayer groups and communities more effective instruments of bringing new people into life in the Spirit.

c. Charismatic Renewal is not limited to the "movement."
The "movement" is still an important vehicle for linking the prayer group and diocesan expressions of the Charismatic Renewal.
- Those of us still active in serving in National Service Committees, Diocesan Service Committees and prayer groups are involved in the "movement."
- However, many who trace the beginning of their life in communities and schools of evangelization to the Charismatic Renewal no longer network

through the movement but through various groupings of communities and associations of evangelization.
- Still others baptized in the Spirit through the vehicle of the Charismatic movement are exercising charisms serving the Church in other ways, even in other movements.

"Baptism in the Holy Spirit is captive to no camp, whether liberal or conservative. Nor is it identified with any one movement, nor with one style of prayer, worship or community. On the contrary we believe that this gift of the baptism in the Holy Spirit belongs to the Christian inheritance of all those sacramentally initiated into the church" (*Fanning the Flame,* p.10).

2. Vision of Charismatic Renewal — what it is.

To quote Cardinal Suenens again, "The soul of Renewal — Baptism in the Spirit — is a grace of pentecostal refreshment offered to all Christians" (article as above).

a. The aims of the Catholic Charismatic Renewal are not different from the objectives of Church — the conversion, sanctification, and empowerment of every human being.

The Bishops of the USA in their 30th Anniversary Statement on the Charismatic Renewal wrote, "It is our conviction that baptism in the Spirit, understood as the reawakening in Christian experience of the presence and action of the Holy Spirit given in Christian initiation, and manifested in a broad range of charisms, including those closely associated with the Catholic Charismatic Renewal, is part of the normal Christian life" (*Grace for a New Springtime*).

b. It has the distinctive call of highlighting the role of the Holy Spirit in the work of conversion, sanctification and empowerment.

- **Conversion and sanctification** — The promise of the Spirit is to "know" the outpouring of God's love (see Rom 5:5), to know Jesus as Savior and to be able to say "Jesus is Lord" (1 Cor 12:3). Pope John Paul II has called "the thirst for holiness one of the most important results of this spiritual re-awakening" (Address to ICCRS, March 1992).
- We risk losing the fire of the Spirit if we lose our hunger, our thirst, and our awareness of our need of more of the Spirit.
- **Sanctification and empowerment** — The promise of the Spirit is to make us "a people" (see Jer 31:31-34), to be of "one mind and one heart" as the apostles were after Pentecost (see Acts 4:32) (NAB).
- We can stifle the fire of Pentecost if we let disunity go unresolved.

- **Empowerment**—The promise of the Spirit is to equip us for mission. "You will receive the power of the Holy Spirit which will come on you, and then you will be my witnesses not only in Jerusalem but throughout Judaea and Samaria, and indeed to earth's remotest end" (Acts 1:8). Again, the Holy Father has affirmed the Charismatic Renewal for its contribution to the re-evangelization of society (Address, ICCRS 1992).
- We can lose the fire of the Holy Spirit if we do not say "yes" to our mission, using the charismatic gifts and calling new people into service.

C. The Mission of the Catholic Charismatic Renewal in the Church and the world

"The Renewal is at its best when, from its internal prayerful reflection, it looks outward to the lives of the many, both churched and unchurched…. Baptism in the Holy Spirit **is** empowerment of individuals and of the Church for its mission in the world" (*Grace for a New Springtime*).

1. Leaven—The Charismatic Renewal is called to be leaven to the "churched" bringing **love** through a new experience of the Holy Spirit and charisms.
a. Keep our focus on baptism in the Holy Spirit and charisms, on the grace not the movement. We are meant to build the kingdom not a movement.
b. Eliminate exclusive talk, for example, asking a fellow parishioner, "Are you born again?"
c. Make sure our prayer meetings and community gatherings are clinics to bring others new life in the Spirit, not clubs that separate us.

2. Light—The Charismatic Renewal is gifted to be a light to the "unchurched," bringing **hope** through healing.
a. We are empowered with charisms to bring healing through prayer groups that are bridges to alienated Catholics, to the hurt, to the disillusioned.
b. Be examples of unity and instruments of reconciliation.

3. Salt—The Charismatic Renewal is sent to be salt to the unconverted, the unevangelized bringing **faith** through effective and creative evangelization.
c. The church calls us to "put out into the deep" (*Novo Millenio Ineunte,* 1).
- We are commissioned to launch out into the ocean not to be satisfied with fishing off the pier.

D. Some Challenges to the Catholic Charismatic Renewal

1. The Catholic Charismatic Renewal can move from the Spirit into the flesh if we fail to balance structure and spontaneity.

In some places there is too much structure, too much formality, and a loss of spontaneity, "guidelines" that dominate the Spirit, stifle the gifts, and hinder evangelization.

- Structure needs to be like the skeleton is to the body; it is there but not too prominent. We don't embrace someone's skeleton.

In other places there is the tendency to treat order as an enemy of the Spirit, to neglect discerning "anointings" of the Spirit, mistaking excessive emotionalism for authentic movements of God, assuming all emotional outbursts are signs of deliverance.

- Without the skeleton the body is formless and out of control. Without order and discernment of spirits the gifts of the Spirit are powerless.

2. We can limit the fire of the Spirit if we fail to balance being fully Catholic, charismatic and integrated into the Church.

a. Be fully charismatic without being separatists, without isolating ourselves from one another's charisms for the Church.

- We can't be like frozen dinners that keep the vegetables separate from the potatoes, separate from the meat and gravy! We can't keep the charismatics here in this compartment, and Marriage Encounter people here and Rosary Society people there.

b. Be fully integrated into the Church without losing our particular charisms for the Church.

- We can't become vegetable juice where the vegetables are so blended together they lose their unique flavor.

c. Keep our unique charisms for the Church while being integrated with other works of the Spirit in the Church.

- We need to be like "stew" where the vegetables are mixed up with the potatoes and meat, all flavoring one another.

3. We can limit the fire of the Spirit if we fail to balance being integrated into the Church and ecumenically open.

a. Be fully Catholic without being closed to ecumenism.

Baptism in the Holy Spirit is an "ecumenical grace."

- Fear from bad experiences in the past can lead to stifling the Spirit moving throughout the whole body of Christ.

b. On the other hand authentic ecumenism does not mean losing our identity. Mary, Peter (the Pope) and the Sacraments are integral to our identity as Catholics.
- Avoid adopting non-Catholic theology and vocabulary.

4. We can move from the Spirit into the flesh if leaders fail to call new people into service and if new people fail to respond.

a. Aging Leaders that are staying in leadership too long, failing to call new people into service, are stifling growth in the Spirit.
- They are standing in "yesterday's anointing" of the Lord for them. They need to move on to the new anointing, so others can move into the service they move out of. There is a direct connection between people being called into service and the degree of their commitment.

b. On the other hand, newer people need to recognize they will grow in the Spirit as they serve.
- Service is not a reward for holiness, but a means to holiness. The Lord ministers to us as we minister to one another.

Session 9
More Wisdom Through Hope

> May he enlighten the eyes of your mind so that you can see what hope his call holds for you, how rich is the glory of the heritage he offers among his holy people (Eph 1:18).

Goals
1. To understand that the Spirit gives us here only a glimpse of the eternal inheritance that we hope for.
2. To accept the call to Hope as the way to experience the full inheritance that Jesus has won for us.

Framing Story
During a time of religious persecution of Catholics, when they were forbidden to publicly celebrate the Holy Sacrifice of the Mass, they met in secret in the early hours of the morning. One morning a soldier stopped a young girl as she went to the celebration of the Eucharist. He asked her, "Where are you going?" She knew she couldn't tell a lie, but she knew if she said where she was going she would be persecuted as well as the people she was going to join. She took a chance that the soldier didn't know the meaning of the Mass. She said to him, "My brother has died. I am going to hear the reading of the will and to claim my inheritance." He let her go. On the way back he stopped her again and asked, "How did you do"? She replied, "He left it all to me!"

Jesus our brother has died, He has left us a rich inheritance and He has left it all to every one of us!

Key Point
Jesus has made us heirs of a rich inheritance. We need the Holy Spirit to claim the first fruits of our inheritance and hope to move us on in the Spirit to the full and eternal experience of what we hope for.

In preparing us for the jubilee year our Holy Father, John Paul II, urged, "Believers should be called to a renewed appreciation of the theological virtue of hope" (*Tertio Millennio Adveniente*, 46).

A. The Spirit leads us to hope.
1. The Spirit leads us to an understanding of hope.

The new Catholic Catechism defines hope as "the theological virtue by which we desire the kingdom of heaven and eternal life as our happiness, placing our trust in Christ's promises and relying not on our own strength, but on the help of the grace of the Holy Spirit" (*CCC*, 1817).

St. Paul wrote to Titus: "By means of the cleansing water of rebirth and renewal in the Holy Spirit which he has so graciously poured over us through Jesus Christ our Saviour ... so that, justified by his grace, we should become heirs in hope of eternal life" (3:5-7).

a. Hope is about desire for a future good that is not yet attained but which is possible to attain.

b. Hope is "the anchor our souls have" (Heb 6:19).
- The anchor by itself is small and powerless. The strength of the anchor is in the ground that it grasps. The strength of our hope is the faithfulness of God.

c. The ground of our hope is the faithfulness of God to His promises. "Let us keep firm in the hope we profess, because the one who made the promise is trustworthy" (Heb 10:23).
- A sure sign of His faithfulness is that "The Father…has given us a new birth into a living hope through the resurrection of Jesus Christ from the dead and into a heritage that can never be spoilt or soiled and never fade away" (1 Pt 1:3-4).

2. The Spirit gives us a foretaste of our inheritance.

"We too, who have the first-fruits of the Spirit ... In hope, we already have salvation; in hope, not visibly present, or we should not be hoping ... But having this hope for what we cannot yet see, we are able to wait for it with persevering confidence" (Rom 8:23-25).

a. It is through the Spirit we come to experience a foretaste of what is to come. This foretaste is real heart knowledge of the fullness that is to come in eternity.

b. Hope is both near and distant!
- It is near because the means—the anchor—to attain the object of desire is near. It is distant because the object of desire—the ground—is distant and unseen. The "eye" of the anchor does not discern what the claws of the anchor grasp to hold the ship safe from the pounding surf.

c. What is near is the foretaste; what is distant is the fullness of the fulfillment of the promises.
- The intensity of hope depends on the closeness of the object hoped for. If I

desire a piece of pumpkin pie the desire is greater if the pie is in the oven, than if the pumpkin is in the garden.

d. The "first-fruits" increase our desire
- They move us beyond a "grin and bear it" attitude to confident assurance that what we hope for can be obtained.
- Let the foretaste call us to new desire, new expectation of the more the Lord has for us.
- "The virtue of hope responds to the aspiration to happiness which God has placed in the heart of every man" (*CCC*, 1818).

3. The Spirit gives us the first fruits of:
a. Our knowing God's love—"Hope…will not let us down, because the love of God has been poured into our hearts by the Holy Spirit" (Rom 5:5).
- Lend your imagination to the Lord. Remember your moment closest to the Lord and realize it is only a shadow of the fullness. Imagine what our day would be like if we were filled with a conviction of His love.

b. Our knowing Jesus as Lord—"Nobody is able to say, 'Jesus is Lord' except in the Holy Spirit" (1 Cor 12:3).
- Remember the relief of surrendering burdens to Him, realizing we don't have to carry them alone. Imagine what our day would be like if we began it with confident assurance that He would take care of all our needs, carry our burdens with us.

c. Our knowing Jesus as Savior—We are "justified by the free gift of his grace through being set free in Christ Jesus" (Rom 3:24).
- Imagine what our day would be like if we had a confidence that there is no darkness within or around us over which He has not won the victory.

d. Our experiencing new gifts—"The gifts that we have differ according to the grace that was given to each of us" (Rom 12:6).
- Imagine the effect of our ministry if we tapped the plentitude of His gifts.

B. Hope deepens life in the Spirit.
1. Hope releases the power of God to act in us.
"'Blessed is she who believed that the promises made her by the Lord would be fulfilled'" (Lk 1:45).

a. Hope is more than believing in His faithfulness, it is trusting in His faithfulness.
Trust goes beyond believing in the head. It is surrendering our life to what we believe.

- A cyclist rode his bicycle on a wire strung across a deep ravine. He asked a spectator, "Do you believe I can ride my bicycle back again?" The spectator replied, "Of course I believe it. I just saw it." That is faith. The cyclist said, "If you really believe it, get on the back!" That is trust.

b. Hope calls for abandonment, for letting go of our power in order to surrender to His power.
- In the Acts of the Apostles, when Paul was given a chance to state his defense, he could have answered by giving an account of his raising the dead, healing the sick, escaping prison, surviving shipwreck. Instead he went to the heart of what he knew was the source of the power of all that he did. "'It is for my hope in the promise made by God to our ancestors that I am on trial'" (Acts 26:6).

2. The Spirit removes the enemies of hope.
"May the God of hope fill you with all joy and peace in your faith, so that in the power of the Holy Spirit you may be rich in hope" (Rom 15:13).

a. Despair is ceasing to hope for salvation, for forgiveness.
- It is experiencing our sinfulness and looking at our selves not Jesus. Judas' response to his sin was despair not repentance, and it led to death.
- It is looking at circumstances without faith. The disciples of Emmaus heard of the empty tomb but instead of remembering the promise of Jesus to rise from the dead they despairingly assumed someone had stolen his body.

b. Presumption is hoping to obtain forgiveness without our efforts.
- It is swinging from the extreme of depending on our efforts, our will power alone, to presuming on God's mighty power and His mercy.
- It is failing to realize that God empowers our will to do what we cannot do of our own efforts.

c. Fear paralyzes us and keeps us closed, unable to hope in His promises.
- Fear of God, of what He might ask, because we don't trust He can put into our hearts His very own desires for us.
- Fear of ourselves, of revealing our poverty and sinfulness, because we don't trust He will continue to love us as we are, here and now, through and through.
- Fear of others, of loving again and being vulnerable again, because we don't trust that God can make our relationships new and heal again the effects of the conflicts that will arise.

3. Hope carries us through purification.
When the water is shallow the anchor can "see" the ground beneath it. As the ship moves deeper into the ocean, the journey of the anchor gets longer and it needs to move through dark waters to grasp the ground that it cannot see.

As we move on in the spiritual journey hope, too, is challenged to move beyond what is seen to what is unseen.

a. Hope goes beyond feeling. In hope we choose to act on faith not feeling.

b. With hope we have unshakeable confidence in the basic promise, "'I am with you always; yes, to the end of time'" (Mt 28:20). Our faithfulness rests on His faithfulness.

c. Hope is also a weapon against the evil one. "Put on…the hope of salvation for a helmet" (1 Thes 5:8).
- St. Therese's little way of spiritual childhood is complete confidence in His faithfulness even in darkness.

C. Patience brings us to the promise of the Spirit we hope for.
"Be patient … Think of a farmer: how patiently he waits for the precious fruit of the ground … You too must be patient; do not lose heart, because the Lord's coming will be soon" (Jas 5:7-8).

Patience is the daily practice of hope and it is a fruit of the Spirit.

1. Patience with God's plan
- It is the patience of Jesus in the passion, accepting suffering for the sake of the kingdom: "'Take this cup away from me. Nevertheless, let your will be done, not mine'" (Lk 22:42).
- It is the patience of waiting, not knowing what God is doing and why. "Those who hope in Yahweh will regain their strength, they will sprout wings like eagles" (Is 40:31).

2. Patience with one another
- It is forbearance under provocation. Jesus gave us an example of patience with one another when He heard Peter denying Him three times. He looked straight at Peter with a look of forgiveness and patience (Lk 22:61).
- The cross of Jesus was our sins and our cross is often the sins of others against us. Living in the Spirit produces the fruit of patience in us so that we can respond with the patience and mercy of Jesus.

3. Patience with ourselves
- It is patience with personal trials confidently believing that "hardship develops perseverance, and perseverance develops a tested character, something that gives us hope" (Rom 5:3).

- Patience with prayer and spiritual life knowing that dryness increases thirst and keeps us seeking the God of Consolation and not the consolation of God.
- Hope is not the absence of adversity. It is courage in the midst of adversity.

St. Elizabeth Seton, whose life was filled with suffering, once said, "There can be no sadness, no disappointment when the soul's only desire is to fulfill the will of God." Or, as St. Paul said, "be joyful in hope, persevere in hardship; keep praying regularly" (Rom 12:12).

Discussion Starters for Sharing Groups

Session 1. Expecting More of the Fire of the Holy Spirit

1. In what ways do you recognize that you limit the outpouring of the Spirit in your life?

2. What obstacles do you need to overcome to receive more of the Spirit?

3. How can you allow the Holy Spirit to stretch you, to empty you, to heal you to receive more of the Spirit?

Session 2. More Love Through Prayer

1. What truth of God's love do you need to let the Holy Spirit reveal to you?

2. What obstacles to experiencing His love in prayer do you need the Holy Spirit to remove?

3. What choices do you need to make in your prayer so that the Holy Spirit can release His power in you in a new way?

Session 3. More Love Through Purification

There are going to be some valleys for all of us. The basic question is not whether we have many or few valleys. It is not whether those valleys are dark or dimly lit.

The questions are:

1. Do you know and accept with surety that it is only through the valleys that you can possibly travel on to higher ground with God?

2. How do you react to them? How do you go through them? Do you face them calmly with Christ? With His gracious Spirit to guide me, do you face them fearlessly?

3. What is God teaching you through suffering? How is He purifying you?

Session 4. More Power Through the Charisms

1. What factors that stifle the charisms do you recognize in yourself and in your prayer group?

2. How are you encouraging, discerning and affirming the charisms of one another? What will you do to improve in this area?

3. Share your experience of using the charisms in your everyday life?

Session 5. More Power Through Community

1. How have you experienced the need for community?

2. Take time to have each person share a personal experience of how God has acted in his or her life.

3. Practice listening to and encouraging one another.

Session 6. More Power Through Service

1. Which point about the zeal of Jesus and the early Church stirred you to new zeal? How?

2. What fear of evangelizing do you recognize in yourself? How will you overcome it?

3. Share one practical way you can become more effectively evangelistic.

Session 7. More Wisdom Through Discernment

1. Share how one of the attitudes for conforming to God's will has been a help or a stumbling block for you in your past experience of discerning God's will.

2. Give some examples in your own life of ordinary and charismatic inspirations.

3. Discuss the difference between the objective and subjective criteria for discernment and the difference between the life of discernment and the charismatic gift of discernment.

Session 8. More Wisdom Through Vision

1. What misunderstandings of the Mission of the Catholic Charismatic Renewal have you encountered in your area? How can we clarify in the Church what is essential in the Catholic Charismatic Renewal?

2. Share about how your area has dealt with one of the challenges to the Catholic Charismatic Renewal raised in the session talk.

3. What other challenges facing the Catholic Charismatic Renewal have you encountered?

Session 9. More Wisdom Through Hope

1. Reflect on how you have grown in an understanding of the relationship between the Holy Spirit and Hope.

2. Share about the enemies of hope that you struggle with.

3. Acknowledge the area of patience that you most need to grow in and pray with one another for the spiritual fruit of patience.

Questions for Personal Reflection

Unit One: More Love
Session 1: Expecting More of the Fire of the Holy Spirit

1. I first experienced being baptized in the Holy Spirit in _____(year), at _____ (group/parish/community).

   I was seeking the baptism in the Holy Spirit because

2. Other important experiences of the infilling of the Holy Spirit in my life have been:

3. The three words/phrases I would use to describe my personal experience of Pentecost are

   _____

   _____

   _____

4. The most accurate way to describe my present desire for more of the Holy Spirit is

   _____ a thimble
   _____ a container filled with many things
   _____ a really larger container filled with holes
   _____ a container constantly being filled and poured out
   _____ another image _____

5. Obstacles that are limiting the outpouring of the Holy Spirit in my life are

   _____ worries about _____
   _____ riches such as _____
   _____ seeking pleasures such as _____

_____ having a difficult time with ongoing repentance
_____ having a difficult time surrendering more of my life to the Lord
_____ other _____

Unit One: More Love
Session 2: More Love Through Prayer

1. I find it easy to believe that God

    _____ loves me personally
    _____ knows my name and calls me by my name
    _____ woos and pursues me
    _____ love me unconditionally, no matter what
    _____ God's love for me is everlasting

2. I find it difficult to believe that God

    _____ loves me personally
    _____ knows my name and calls me by my name
    _____ woos and pursues me
    _____ love me unconditionally, no matter what
    _____ God's love for me is everlasting

3. I give thanks to the Holy Spirit for removing these obstacles to experiencing the love of God in prayer

    _____ failure to be still
    _____ having an image of God as avenging judge
    _____ putting myself under condemnation because of sin
    _____ avoiding painful questions
    _____ failure to come to God with my sin
    _____ failure to come to God with my troubles
    _____ failure to come to God with my distractions
    _____ failure to come to God with my sickness and be sick with Him

There's Always More: Expecting New Fire   93

4. I need the help of the Holy Spirit for removing these obstacles to experiencing the love of God in prayer

   _____ failure to be still
   _____ having an image of God as avenging judge
   _____ putting myself under condemnation because of sin
   _____ avoiding painful questions
   _____ failure to come to God with my sin
   _____ failure to come to God with my troubles
   _____ failure to come to God with my distractions
   _____ failure to come to God with my sickness and be sick with Him

5. To become more available to, vulnerable to and expectant of God's power being released in my prayer life, I will begin to

   _____ give God prime time
   _____ find a regular time for personal prayer
   _____ spend _____ minutes in prayer each day
   _____ extend my spontaneous worship
   _____ spend time reading Scripture each day
   _____ make intercession a regular part of my daily prayer

Unit One: More Love
Session 3: More Love Through Purification

1. When suffering occurs in my life, I usually react by saying:

   _____ Why me?
   _____ What did I do wrong to be punished in this way?
   _____ All suffering is bad.
   _____ Suffering is a cross that I must bear.
   _____ All suffering must be healed.
   _____ Suffering draws me closer to God.
   _____ I just resign myself to the suffering.
   _____ I join my suffering to the suffering of Christ for the sake of others.
   _____ Lord, what are you trying to teach me through this suffering?

2. An experience of "darkness" (physical pain, emotional turmoil, spiritual dryness) that has actually been "light" showing me the way to God is

3. Thinking over the past three sessions: In order to experience the more love promised by God through expecting, prayer and purification, I ask the members of my sharing group to prayer with me for

Unit Two: More Power
Session 4: More Power Through the Charisms

1. Since being baptized in the Holy Spirit I have gratefully received and exercised these charisms in my life for the sake of building the Body of Christ and the Kingdom of God

    _____ tongues   _____ prophecy   _____ healing
    _____ teaching   _____ preaching   _____ faith
    _____ giving   _____ mercy   _____ helping
    _____ administration   _____ intercession   _____ hospitality
    _____ words of wisdom and knowledge   _____ voluntary poverty

    Think of a few specific times outside a prayer meeting setting when receiving and exercising charisms has brought the blessing and power of the Lord to others and to yourself.

2. The charisms are being stifled in myself or my prayer group because

    _____ of a general lack of desire
    _____ some charisms are not valued
    _____ I/we don't foster their working together
    _____ I/we don't accept our mission to evangelize
    _____ I/we are limiting charisms to certain people
    _____ of a too narrow view of what are charisms
    _____ I/we are over-emphasizing the exercise of charisms at the prayer meeting and not encouraging their use in everyday life.

There's Always More: Expecting New Fire

_____ I/we equate charisms with being young in the Spirit and not for the maturity we are now seeking
_____ I/we are not providing correction (pruning) in the use of charisms

3. Receiving and exercising charisms is being encouraged and affirmed in our group by

   _____ providing regular teaching about charisms
   _____ praying regularly with people to being open to the Holy Spirit and the charisms
   _____ working with prayer group members, individually and in small groups, to discern the charisms God is giving to them
   _____ working to build greater unity in the prayer group
   _____ giving regular feedback to people when they have exercised charisms so they can grow in the use of them

Unit Two: More Power
Session 5: More Power Through Community

1. I have become most aware of my need for community through

   _____ reflecting on the meaning of my Baptism
   _____ reflecting on Jesus' example of calling disciples to "be with him"
   _____ understanding Jesus' New Commandment: "Love one another as I have loved you."
   _____ understanding St. Paul's teaching about the Body of Christ
   _____ my own human need

2. I have experienced being loved in community as others

   _____ cared for me when I was weak
   _____ really listened to me
   _____ showed me compassion
   _____ encouraged me

_____ shared their lives with me, were vulnerable
_____ forgave me
_____ spoke the truth to me in love; admonished me
_____ showed me patience

Think of one or two specific examples when you experienced love in community.

3. I have tried to build community by

    _____ caring for others when they were weak
    _____ really listening to others
    _____ showing compassion
    _____ encouraging others
    _____ sharing my life with others, being vulnerable
    _____ forgiving others
    _____ speaking the truth in love; admonishing others
    _____ showing others patience

    Think of one or two specific examples when you were a community-builder.

4. A time when I was really listened to was

    What about this person made me feel like I was listened to:

5. Take a few minutes in the sharing group or later to thank God for the times when you experienced His love through community and for the times you felt listened to.

    Pray for and, if necessary, forgive those people who failed to show the love you needed, didn't listen when you were sharing something important.

Unit Two: More Power
Session 6: More Power Through Service

1. I am stirred up to serve when I

    _____ see the example of Jesus' zeal
    _____ read Jesus' command to go and evangelize
    _____ think about the example of the early Church from the Acts of the Apostles
    _____ read about the lives of the saints
    _____ see the example of people today.

    A specific example that makes me want to give my all in service for the Kingdom of God is

2. I sometimes hesitate sharing my faith with others because

    _____ I feel inadequate; I know I am no saint
    _____ I fear that I will fail; what if people don't accept the message I bring?
    _____ I don't want people to think I believe I am better than they are
    _____ I don't want to "pay the price" of my time, energy for getting involved
    _____ I'm afraid that people will reject me, think less of me, ridicule me

3. Despite my fears, I have shared my faith with others. A time when this sharing went particularly well was

4. A thumbnail sketch of a personal witness is
    [This could be a witness of your turning to God for the first time. Or, it could be a witness of a change in your life, for example, away from anger, from fear to calm, from not liking yourself to a healthy self-image, from bitterness to forgiveness. Or, it could be a witness in your spiritual life related to growth in prayer, reading the Bible, confession, attending Mass, praying the Rosary.]

My life before God touched me

What Jesus in the power of the Spirit did for me

The difference that this made in my life was

5. Thinking over the past three sessions: In order to experience the more power promised by God through charisms, community and service I ask the members of my sharing group to prayer with me for

Unit Three: More Wisdom
Session 7: More Wisdom Through Discernment

1. What makes it hard for me to hear/conform to God's will for me are

    _____ the faith that God wants me to know His will for my life
    _____ spending enough time in prayer
    _____ having the attitude that I'll obey God's will even before I know what it is
    _____ surrendering my whole life to God, wanting to hold onto doing things my way in some areas of my life
    _____ making enough time for recollection: in prayer, about the circumstances of my life, about words of inspiration or prophecies
    _____ waiting on the Lord, being impetuous

2. I have experienced God guiding my life through

    _____ reading the Scripture in personal prayer
    _____ the teaching of the Church
    _____ the general life direction/vocation to which God has called me.
    _____ the Scripture read at Mass or at a prayer meeting
    _____ the counsel of a friend or spiritual director

_____ the circumstances of my life
_____ ordinary inspirations/inner urgings
_____ charismatic inspirations (dreams/visions/prophetic words)

3. I have tested inspirations in my life most effectively through

_____ experiencing a deep sense of peace
_____ checking whether I am motivated by love
_____ being reassured by joy
_____ relating it to the Word of God
_____ allowing God to work through circumstances
_____ submitting to the discernment of community

4. Choose one or two of the instances of trying to discern God's will in your life and write briefly about them: how did God "speak" to you?; how did you discern the prompting of God?; how did you know if your discernment was correct?

Unit Three: More Wisdom
Session 8: More Wisdom Through Vision

Questions 1-5 for all, 6-7 for those in prayer groups, communities, etc.

1. Check the misunderstandings of the Catholic Charismatic Renewal that you have encountered.

_____ the Charismatic Renewal was founded by a group of students in Pittsburgh, U.S.A. in 1967.
_____ the Charismatic Renewal is a spirituality just for some people like Franciscan spirituality is for others.
_____ the Charismatic Renewal is like other organizations with a specific chief executive and an administrative structure.
_____ the Charismatic Renewal is a form of prayer for those who like to raise their hands when they pray.
_____ it is for emotional people.

2. What do you understand now is the purpose of the Catholic Charismatic Renewal?

3. Is everyone who is charismatic involved in the Charismatic "movement"? Explain.

4. If you are not currently in a prayer group, community or School of Evangelization, how do you see yourself bringing your new life in the Spirit to the people of God in your personal life?

5. What challenges do you expect to encounter?

6. If you attend a prayer group, community, or School of Evangelization, write a sentence describing the vision of the group, including its identity and mission.

7. Indicate on the lines below where your group is in terms of the challenges to find balance in the Catholic Charismatic Renewal.

Structure	Balance	Spontaneity
Fully Charismatic	Balance	Fully Catholic
Separatist: Remains apart	Balance	Integrated with parish/diocese
Ecumenically closed	Balance	Ecumenically open
Leaders calling new people forth	Balance	Leaders not calling new people forth
New people responding to the call to service	Balance	New people not responding to the call to service

Unit Three: More Wisdom
Session 9: More Wisdom Through Hope

1. A time when I experienced hope as an anchor—both the near and far of it—was

2. I have experienced "getting on the back" of God, of trusting in His faithfulness. It was when

3. I continue to struggle with these enemies of hope

    _____ experiencing my sinfulness, especially at habits of sin, and despairing
    _____ looking at the circumstances of my life and not being able to hear or remember the promises of Christ
    _____ fear
    _____ needing always to see, to feel instead of choosing to act on faith
    _____ impatience, wanting everything to happen immediately

4. Thinking over the past three sessions: In order to experience the more wisdom promised by God through discernment, vision and hope I ask the members of my sharing group to prayer with me for

Growth Seminar Additional Resources

Preparation for Teachers

Boucher, Therese. *The New Life in the Spirit Seminars Team Manual: Catholic Edition 2000.* Locust Grove, VA: National Service Committee, 2000.

Catechism of the Catholic Church. Liguori, MO: Liguori Publications, 1994.

Kellar, Sr. Nancy, S.C., editor. *The Vocation of a Leader: Called, Gifted and Sent,* Collection of articles from Leadership Formation Insert. Vatican City, Europe: ICCRS Newsletter, ICCRS, 1998.

Pentecost Today. Locust Grove, VA: National Service Committee.

Pesare, Oreste, editor. *Then Peter Stood Up...*, Collection of the Popes' Addresses to the Catholic Charismatic Renewal from its origin to the year 2000. Vatican City, Europe: ICCRS, 2000.

Session 1. Expecting More of the Fire of the Holy Spirit

Cantalamessa, Fr. Raniero, O.F.M.Cap. *The Holy Spirit in the Life of Jesus.* Collegeville, MN: Liturgical Press, 1994.

Montague, Fr. George, S. M. *The Holy Spirit: Growth of a Biblical Tradition.* New York, NY: Paulist Press, 1976.

Montague, Fr. George, S.M. *Still Riding the Wind.* Mineola, NY: Resurrection Press, 1994.

Martin, Fr. Francis, editor. *Baptism in the Holy Spirit: Reflections on a Contemporary Grace in the Light of the Catholic Tradition.* St Bede's Publications, 1998.

McDonnell, Fr. Kilian, and Montague, Fr. George. *Christian Initiation and Baptism in the Holy Spirit.* Collegeville, MN: Liturgical Press, 1991.

McDonnell, Fr. Kilian, and Montague, Fr. George, editors. *Fanning the Flame: What Does Baptism in the Holy Spirit Have to Do with Christian Initiation?* Collegeville, MN: Liturgical Press, 1991.

McKinney, Bishop Joseph, and Poat, Angie. *Perpetuating Pentecost.* USA: Published by the authors, 2000.

National Conference of Catholic Bishops. *Grace for the New Springtime.* Washington, DC: United States Catholic Conference, 1997.

Pope John Paul II. *Dominum Et Vivificantem (The Holy Spirit in the Life of the Church and the World)*. Boston, MA: Pauline Books, 1986.

Theological-Historical Commission for the Great Jubilee of the Year 2000. *The Holy Spirit, Lord and Giver of Life*. New York, NY: Crossroad Publishing Company, 1997.

Session 2. More Love Through Prayer

Barry, Fr. William, S.J. *What Do I Want in Prayer?* New York, NY: Paulist Press, 1974.

Bloom, Anthony, Bp. *Beginning to Pray*. Paulist Press, New York, NY, 1970.

Cantalamessa, Fr. Raniero, O.F.M.Cap. *Life in the Lordship of Jesus*. Mumbai, India: St. Pauls, 1990.

Faricy, Fr. Robert, S.J. *Lord, Teach Us to Pray*. Vatican City, Europe: ICCRS, 1998.

Farrell, Fr. Edward. *The Father is Very Fond of Me*. Denville, NJ: Dimension Books, 1975.

Kreeft, Peter. *Knowing the Truth of God's Love*. Ann Arbor, MI: Servant Books, 1988.

Martin, George. *To Pray As Jesus Did*. Ann Arbor, MI: Servant Books, 1978.

Martin, Ralph. *Hungry for God*. Ann Arbor, MI: Servant Books.

Ten Boom, Corrie. *The Hiding Place*. Old Tappan, NJ: Spire Books, 1971.

Theological-Historical Commission for the Great Jubilee of the Year 2000. *God, the Father of Mercy*. New York, NY: Crossroad Publishing Company, 1998.

Theological-Historical Commission for the Great Jubilee of the Year 2000. *Jesus Christ, Word of the Father*. New York, NY: Crossroad Publishing Company, 1997.

Session 3. More Love Through Purification

Boughton, Rosemary. *Praying With Teresa of Avila*. Winona, MN: Saint Mary's Press, 1990.

Green, Fr. Thomas, S. J. *When the Well Runs Dry*. Notre Dame, IN: Ave Maria Press, 1979.

Keller, Philip. *A Shepherd Looks at Psalm 23*. Grand Rapids, MI: Zondervan, 1970.

Kreeft, Peter. *Making Sense Out of Suffering*. Ann Arbor, MI: Servant Books, 1986.

Kosicki, Fr. George, C.S.B. *The Good News of Suffering*. Grand Rapids, MI: Liturgical Press, 1981.

Lewis, C.S. *The Problem of Pain*. New York, NY: Macmillan Publishing Co., 1978.

Pope John Paul II. *Salvifici Doloris (On the Christian Meaning of Human Suffering)*. Boston, MA: Paulist Books, 1984.

Session 4. More Power Through the Charisms

Clark, Steve. *Baptized in the Spirit and Spiritual Gifts*. Pecos, NM: Dove Publications, 1969.

Coughlin, Father Peter. *Understanding the Charismatic Gifts*.

DeGrandis, Fr. Robert, SSJ. *Charisms-Gifts of God's Love*. Hauppauge, NJ: Living Flame, 1997.

Kellar, Sr. Nancy and Thorp, David. *Charisms: Stirring Up the Gifts of the Spirit*, Video Series. Locust Grove, VA: Chariscenter USA, 1988.

Sullivan, Fr. Francis, S.J. *Charisms and the Charismatic Renewal*. Ann Arbor, MI: Servant Books, 1982.

Yocum, Bruce. *Prophecy*. Ann Arbor, MI: Servant Publications, 1976, revised, 1998.

Session 5. More Power Through Community

Aridas, Fr. Chris. *Reconciliation*. Garden City, NY: Image Books, 1987.

Delespesse, Fr. Max. *The Church Community Leaven and Life-style*. Ottawa, Canada: Catholic Center, St. Paul University, 1968.

Dubay, Fr. Thomas, S. M. *Caring: A Biblical Theology of Community*. Denville, NJ: Dimension Books, 1973.

Kellar, Sr. Nancy, SC and Wirth, Sr. Justin, SSND. *Faith Sharing in Small Groups*. Locust Grove, VA: Chariscenter USA, 1990, revised, 2002.

Kellar, Sr. Nancy and Thorp, David. *Unity: Building Relationships,* Video Series. Locust Grove, VA: Chariscenter USA, 1990.

Lee, Fr. Bernard, S.M. editor. *The Catholic Experience of Small Christian Communities.* Mahwah, NJ: Paulist Press, 2000.

Linn, Dennis and Matthew. *Healing of Memories.* New York, NY: Paulist Press, 1974.

MacNutt, Francis. *Healing.* Notre Dame, IN: Ave Maria Press, 1974.

Pope John Paul II. *Christifideles Laici (On the Vocation and the Mission of the Lay Faithful in the Church and the World).* Boston, MA: Pauline Books, 1989.

Scanlon, Fr. Michael, *Inner Healing.* New York, NY: Paulist Press, 1974.

Session 6. More Power Through Service

Aridas, Fr. Chris. *Bringing Christ to My Everyday World,* A School of Evangelization Video Series. Locust Grove, VA: Chariscenter USA, 1990.

Aridas, Fr. Chris, and Boucher, John. *Bringing Prayer Meetings to Life.* Pecos, NM: Dove Publications, 1990.

Blum, Susan. *The Ministry of Evangelization.* Collegeville, MN: Liturgical Press, 1988.

Hater, Fr. Robert J. *News That is Good: Evangelization for Catholics.* Notre Dame, IN: Ave Maria Press, 1990.

Kellar, Sr. Nancy and Thorp, David. *Service: A New Heart/A New Mind,* Video Series. Locust Grove, VA: Chariscenter USA, 1987.

Mansfield, Patti Gallagher. *Proclaim His Marvelous Deeds: How To Give a Personal Witness.* Steubenville, OH: Franciscan University Press, 1987.

Pope John Paul II. *Redemptoris Missio (Mission of the Redeemer).* Boston, MA: Pauline Books, 1992.

Pope John Paul II. *Novo Millenio Ineunte (At the Beginning of a New Millennium).* Boston, MA: Pauline Books, 2001.

Pope Paul VI. *Evangelii Nuntiandi (On Evangelization in the Modern World).* Washington, DC: United States Catholic Conference, 1976.

Ranaghan, Kevin. *In the Power of the Spirit: Effective Catholic Evangelization.* Mineola, NY: Resurrection Press, 1991.

Wilson, Ken. *Decision To Love.* Ann Arbor, MI: Servant Books, 1980.

Session 7. More Wisdom Through Discernment

Aridas, Fr. Chris. *Seeking God in Every Situation.* New York, NY: Living Flame Press, 1981.

Boucher, John. *Following Jesus: A Disciples Guide to Discerning God's Will.* Pecos, MN: Dove Publications, 1995.

Faricy, Fr. Robert, S.J. *Seeking Jesus in Contemplation and Discernment.* Westminster, MD: Christian Classics, Inc., 1987.

Groeschel, Fr. Benedict, C.F.R. *A Still Small Voice.* San Francisco, CA: Ignatius Press, 1993.

Scanlon, Fr. Michael, T.O.R. *What Does God Want?* Huntington, IN: Our Sunday Visitor, Inc., 1996.

Session 8. More Wisdom Through Vision

Cordes, Bishop Paul. *Born of the Spirit: Renewal Movements in the Life of the Church.* South Bend, IN: Greenlawn Press, 1992.

Cordes, Bishop Paul. *Call to Holiness: Reflections on the Catholic Charismatic Renewal.* Collegeville, MN: Liturgical Press, 1997.

Kellar, Sr. Nancy, S.C., editor. *Charismatic Renewal: a Grace, a Challenge and a Mission*, Collection of articles from ICCRS Newsletter. Vatican City, Europe: ICCRS, 2000.

Kellar, Sr. Nancy, SC and Thorp, David. *Maintaining Vibrant Prayer Groups*, Video Series. Locust Grove, VA: Chariscenter USA, 1987.

Mansfield, Patti Gallagher. *As By a New Pentecost: The Dramatic Beginnings of the Catholic Charismatic Renewal.* Steubenville, OH: Franciscan University Press, 1992

McDonnell, Fr. Kilian, O.S.B. editor. *Toward a New Pentecost for a New Evangelization: Malines Document I, Second Edition.* Collegeville, MN: Liturgical Press, 1993.

McDonnell, Fr. Kilian, O.B.S., editor. *Open the Windows: The Popes and the Charismatic Renewal.* South Bend, IN: Greenlawn Press, 1989.

McDonnell, Killian, O.B.S., editor. *The Holy Spirit and Power: The Catholic Charismatic Renewal.* Garden City, NY: Doubleday, 1975.

Martin, Ralph. *The Catholic Church at the End of an Age.* San Francisco, CA: Ignatius Press, 1994.

National Conference of Catholic Bishops. *Grace for the New Springtime.* Washington, DC: United States Catholic Conference, 1997.

Pope John Paul II. *Tertio Millennio Adveniente (Toward the Third Millennium).* Boston, MA: Pauline Books, 1994.

Suenens, Leon Joseph Cardinal. *Memories and Hopes.* Dublin, Ireland: Veritas, 1992.

Session 9. More Wisdom Through Hope

Blattner, John. *Growing in the Fruits of the Spirit.* Ann Arbor, MI: Servant Publications, 1984.

Lee, Richard. *Windows of Hope.* Sisters, OR: Multinomah Press, nd.

Shlemon, Barbara. *Living Each Day by the Power of Faith.* Ann Arbor, MI: Servant Books, 1986.

Valles, Fr. Carlos, S.J. *Models of Faith.* Chicago, IL: Loyola University Press, 1990.

NATIONAL SERVICE COMMITTEE

The National Service Committee is a body of leaders in the Catholic Charismatic Renewal who work together to serve the Lord.

"Catholic Charismatic Renewal invites all people to experience the Holy Spirit who opens us to a life-changing relationship with Jesus Christ and the love of the Father. The Holy Spirit empowers us for personal holiness, renewed Catholic life, and evangelization." (The Vision Statement of the National Service Committee)

Flowing from this vision is the National Service Committee's sense of mission:

> The mission of the National Service Committee is to foster the dynamic grace of baptism in the Holy Spirit (Acts 1:5) which empowered the members of the early Church at Pentecost.

The NSC accomplishes this by:

Proclaiming the Lordship of Jesus Christ and the love of the Father in the power of the Holy Spirit which leads to the renewal of the **grace and culture of Pentecost.**

Encouraging the awareness and the experience of the **full role of the Holy Spirit** among Catholic Charismatic Renewal groups and ministries, with the goal of reminding the Church to be fully conscious of this role.

This action of the Holy Spirit leads to:
- ❖ Experiencing union with God
- ❖ Inner transformation, leading to personal holiness
- ❖ Ministry empowered by the charisms for evangelization and service
- ❖ Building communities that witness to a renewed Catholic life.

Assisting leadership development as well as serving and offering **leadership** to the Renewal.

Cooperating with other **Catholic organizations and movements** as well as other Christian groups in **authentic ecumenism.**

Empowering **youth and young adults** by entering into dialogue with them regarding the Holy Spirit in their lives and inviting them to participate in the Catholic Charismatic Renewal.

NATIONAL SERVICE COMMITTEE RESOURCES

A.C.T.S of Leadership (set of 4 DVDs) $39.95
    Presentations on apostolic, communal, theological and spiritual formation for leaders.

Bringing Christ to My Everyday World School of Evangelism

    3   90 minute videotapes and 10 workbooks $54.95

    5   60 minute audiotapes and 5 workbooks $29.95

Charisms $2.50
    A collection of articles from *Pentecost Today*

Leadership Training DVDs

    - Maintaining Vibrant Prayer Groups $25.00

    - Charisms: Stirring Up the Gifts of the Spirit $25.00

    - Service: A New Heart/A New Mind $25.00

    - Unity: Building Relationships $25.00

The New Life in the Spirit Seminars Team Manual: Catholic Edition 2000 $9.95

A New Pentecost DVD $14.00
    Overview of the Catholic Charismatic Renewal

Nurturing New Life in the Spirit: Training Sessions for the New Life in the Spirit Seminar $34.95
    2 videos and workbook

A Prayer Journal for Baptism in the Holy Spirit $2.50

A Road to Pentecost $2.50
    Brief meditations for Easter to Pentecost

NSC Leaflets $.50

- Catholic Charismatic Renewal Terms and Phrases
- Catholic Charismatic Renewal: Papal Affirmation and Priestly Witness
- Charismatic Prayer Meetings
- Discernment and Discernment of Spirits
- *The Full Role of the Holy Spirit
- The Gifts of the Holy Spirit
- Healing Prayer
- *Introduction to Teachings at Prayer Meetings
- Living Baptized in the Holy Spirit
- Prayer Ministry
- Understanding and Exercising the Gift of Prophecy
- Word of Knowledge and the Word of Wisdom

Great for beginners and veterans alike! The two marked with an * are especially geared for leaders.

All prices in U.S. dollars. Shipping and handling are extra.

Contact: Catholic Charismatic Renewal
              National Service Committee
              Chariscenter USA
              P.O. Box 628
              Locust Grove, VA 22508
              (800) 338-2445
              Fax: (540) 972-0627
              E-mail: chariscenter@nsc-chariscenter.org

Pentecost Today

Working to "foster the dynamic grace of baptism in the Holy Spirit (Acts 1:5) which empowered the members of the early Church at Pentecost," the National Service Committee publishes *Pentecost Today* four times a year.

SEMINAR LEADER

We would be happy to add participants in the Growth Seminar to our mailing list to receive *Pentecost Today* for a year without cost. Please send us their names and addresses and we will gladly add them.

You may send the list by mail, fax or e-mail:

Catholic Charismatic Renewal
National Service Committee
Chariscenter USA
P.O. Box 628
Locust Grove, VA 22508
FAX: (540) 972-0627
e-mail: chariscenter@nsc-chariscenter.org